Dedicado a las mujeres en la lucha

ISBN-13 978-1546857938

ISBN-10 1546857931

Table of Contents: *Life and Labor of a Social Activist and Her Family: A Mexican Story*

Preface

I first met Ernestina in the fall of 1988, some months after I had moved to the colonia Unión de Residentes Lázaro Cárdenas in Mexicali to do my Ph.D. research on patterns of migration to that community. She was president of the colonia (named neighborhood) at that time, and came to introduce herself to me, most probably to find out what I—a foreigner—was doing living in the colonia.

Not long afterwards we became good friends. She was often at my house in the evenings, and I often visited her at her house—when it was still unfinished and had plywood walls and a tarpaulin ceiling. In 1992, with the aid of the Association for Borderlands Studies (ABS) I arranged for five women, four residents of the colonia, to acquire visas to the U.S. Ernestina was among them and presented on women's roles in the establishment of *colonias populares* (working-class squatter settlements) and on work in the informal economy at ABS conferences in Glendale, Arizona (1992) and in Corpus Christi, Texas (1993).

I was very aware of the suffering her husband caused her and of her great efforts to improve the colonia where we lived. There was no running water or sewerage system in the colonia when I arrived there, and Ernestina organized demonstrations at the Civic Center to press the government for these services. I attended these demonstrations, as well as meetings in government offices. I was able to do so because I had a professional visa that let me use the pretext that I was studying Mexicali's *colonias populares* in case my presence was ever challenged. It never was.

At the time of the establishment of Unión de Residentes Lázaro Cárdenas, the World Bank and other international financial institutions were extending loans to many countries, including Mexico, for slum and squatter settlement upgrading. Part of these institutions' motivations—with U.S.—support—was to combat the ungrounded fear that, after the Cuban Revolution, communist agitation might spark unrest and uprisings among the poor who lived in these urban communities (Burgess, 1988: 137-141; Fischer, 2014: 29); Harms, 1992: 22-24).

The Mexican government, especially under the administrations of President de la Madrid (1982-1988) and President Salinas de Gortari (1988-1994), embraced the polices of the World Bank's concentration on self-help housing and squatter settlement regulation in the interests of alleviating poverty (Zanetta, 2004: 39-43) and of legitimizing the political system (Gilbert and Ward, 1985: 201). At that time this latter objective meant keeping the P.R.I. (*Partido Revolucionario Institutional*) in power. When Ernestina had contact with governmental offices in Mexicali, the officials assumed that she was a supporter of that political party, and partially in order to achieve her and her comrades objectives for the colonia, she acquiesced to that identification.

Ernestina's role as a community leader and her women comrades who accompanied her to myriad offices in order to seek legalization of the of the colonia and then to obtain services such as electricity and running water for its residents underscores the importance of women's work in squatter settlement development (see Moser, 1987). While Ernestina achieved much for her colonia, and while she took part in other invasions later on, her personal life left much to be desired. Her husband, Adolfo, mistreated her physically and emotionally and was often unfaithful, eventually abandoning her for another woman. One of the chapters in the book is dedicated to looking at their relationship, but both positive and negative evaluations of her husband's behavior are found in other chapters. Her daughters also suffered physical and/or emotional violence from their partners.

In 2012 I decided I would like to write a book about Ernestina's life, as exemplary of the situation of poor women in Mexico during the past few decades.

Ernestina had been part of the flow of rural to urban migrants so common after World War II: she had been born on a *rancho* (unincorporated rural settlement) in Chihuahua and moved first to Mexico City to work as a domestic servant, and then to various centers in Baja California, on the U.S.-Mexico border. She was part of the urban poor in Mexican cities who invaded lands and self-built housing in order to have a roof over their heads. She was involved in political maneuverings and demonstrations to assure herself and her fellow community residents of property rights and urban services. In her private life she suffered under the reign of machismo.

Though conversations and informal interviews with Ernestina, I filled almost 200 notebook pages. I knew much about her life from conversations we had as friends in the colonia and from her visits to where I live in Los Cabos and in San Diego. When Hurricane Odile hit Los Cabos on September 15, 2014, many of my books, papers, and notebooks were destroyed—including the notebooks from which I hoped to write Ernestina's life story. When Ernestina came to visit me in November of 2014, I told her that we would have to begin again.

But now she took the book into her own hands. Working with three notebooks, she began to write down what she felt was important about her life, making occasional notes between November 2014 and July 2015. She used one to write about her youth and children and migrations, one to write about her first years in Mexicali and selling newspapers, and one to write about the invasion and subsequent development of the colonia where she lives.

Although Ernestina has only completed six years of formal education, her spelling was impeccable. She attributes this to her love of cross-word puzzles—she almost always has a book of them in hand. She also likes reading my books in Spanish on gender relations in Latin America and on the Mexican Revolution.

Once when she got stuck in her writing, I suggested she think of her life as a *novela*—the soap operas that many Mexicans watch on television. From this, I believe, came her presentation of some data in the form of dialogues, especially with her daughters. This, however, is a common way to relate past conversations in Mexico, and it even used among the more educated.

I would put the pages she presented to me each time she came to visit, or wrote while visiting, on the computer, then translate them into English. At the end, I would ask her about anything I knew that might be missing—for example, she had not mentioned the other invasions she had taken part in or discussed what work her offspring did. She left me the responsibility of organizing her writings into chapters.

Ernestina did not write about everything that she experienced or that happened to her. For example, there is nothing about the five different *colonias* where she lived in Mexico City before coming to Rosarito, Baja California, and there is little about her life in Rosarito or in Tijuana. Also omitted is some of the work she engaged in—like harvesting tomatoes outside of Rosarito, taking in sewing in Mexico City and Mexicali, and running a small store in Unión de Residentes Lázaro Cárdenas. What is written is what she considered to be the most important happenings in her life, and about the struggles that defined her.

Tamar Diana Wilson

23 June 2017, Los Cabos, Mexico

References cited

Fischer, Brodwyn

2014. "A Century in the Present Tense: Crisis Politics and the Intellectual History of Brazil's Informal Cities," pp. 9-67 in Brodwyn Fischer, Bryan McCann and Javier Auyero, eds. *Cities from Scratch: Poverty and Informality in Urban Latin America.* Durham: Duke University Press.

Harms, Hans

1982. "Historical Perspectives on the Practice and Purpose of Self-Help Housing," pp. 11-53 in Peter M. Ward, ed. *Self-Help Housing: A Critique.* London: Mansell Publishing Limited.

Gilbert, Alan and Peter M. Ward

1985. *Housing the State, and the Poor: Policy and Practice in Three Latin American Cities.* New York: Cambridge University Press.

Moser, Caroline O.N.

1987. "Women, Human Settlements, and Housing: A Conceptual Framework for Analysis and Policy-Making," pp. 12-32 in Caroline O.N. Moser and Linda Peake, eds. *Women, Human Settlements and Housing.* New York: Tavistock Publications.

Zanetta, Cecilia

2004. *The Influence of the World Bank on National Housing and Urban Politics: The Case of Mexico and Argentina During the 1990s.* Burlington, Vermont: Ashgate.

Chapter I. Youth

This is part of my life. I will write it down as I remember it. Because maybe I do not remember everything, but I will try to mention, little by little, what comes to my memory. And with the little that I will narrate, may it serve as experience for the women who lived something similar to that which happened to me.

Well, I was the daughter of parents who were peasants, originating from the state of Chihuahua, each born on *ranchos* (unincorporated rural settlements). My father was from San Francisco de Conchas, Chihuahua, previously part of the municipality of Ciudad Camargo. Now it has its own municipality. My mother was from a rancho called Subida Alta, municipality of Ciudad Saucillo, Chihuahua. Then my grandmother, mother of my father, moved to Ciudad Saucillo. That is how my parents met.

My paternal grandfather had his own lands. He was married to another *señora*, and my grandmother was his concubine. And my father and his other siblings were born of this concubinage. He was the youngest of his siblings. My grandfather's legitimate children inherited the lands when he died. And since they didn't work the lands they lost them, and later other people invaded them because there was no one to protest.

And so it was that my parents met. And my maternal grandparents established themselves in the *rancho* that I mentioned. They came from the state of Aguascalientes. I never knew from what part of the state. According to my grandfather my grandmother was among those who Pancho Villa brought along with his troops. He told us that my grandmother was one of the women camp followers (*soldaderas*) who came in the northbound train. And they were in charge of making food for his golden ones (*dorados*), as they call his soldiers.

My father was very young and my mother an adolescent. They were 18 and 15 years old when they married, or rather, when they started living together. And they had two sons before I was born, but they died. And when my mother became pregnant with me, she hoped I would be a boy. Because back they there were no ultrasounds to say whether it would be a girl or boy, and even less did they go to see a doctor. All births were attended by midwives. But, oh, what a surprise! I was born female and my mother was very disappointed because she wanted a boy, because she wanted him to be a man and thus able to help my father out in the fields. He always worked as a day laborer for *patrones* [bosses, employers, land owners].

But my father was very happy with me. And it seems he said to my mother, "I have always worked alone. I have never needed anyone to help support you, and don't be distressed. Sons will come along later and we will see if I use them to help me."

I never imagined how great my mother's unhappiness was. She named my brothers who came after me, with the same names as those who had died. She named the oldest Ramón and the other one Isabel. She was a mother of a rather forceful nature, completely the opposite of my father. But she was a mother who protected her children. She never embraced us, but I always felt her protection.

I scarcely remember when I was 3 years old and my brother was born. He was born in Ciudad Juárez. My paternal grandmother took my mother to that city so that he would be born there, and she attended my mother for the birth. Everything went well. I was very little and scarcely realized what was happening. Then my other siblings were born, seven of us. We were born on the various *ranchos* where my father worked. But because I was the eldest, I went with him to pick cotton, or whatever they sowed on the *rancho*, because he had no rest. And it wasn't because my father forced me to go. I cried until he took me. I didn't want to be at home. I was happy at my father's side.

And so I learned to pick cotton, peanuts, tomatoes, and many other things. And above all else I liked eating with him because the bean tacos my mother sent along seemed very tasty to me. And even more when they were heated. And she sent a bottle of black coffee.

He heated the tacos on hot coals. Also, when he finished work in the fields he set about making adobes. And I helped him to mix the mud with wheat straw so that the adobes would be compacted. These times were very nice, because, well, my siblings never liked to go with my father. They stayed at home and did errands for my mother.

And so we grew. Until one day my mother talked to my father, telling him what she thought about their children. She did not want us to remain unschooled. At least we should learn to read and write. And she didn't want us to remain burros (illiterates) like them. And so we went to the town, La Boquilla, the closest town where there was a school. I don't remember the name of the *rancho* where we lived at that time. It was very close to La Boquilla de Conchas. They lived in the town, then on the *rancho*, then again in La Boquilla.

At that time I was 7 years old but I found it very hard to adapt to the life of the town. And even more the first time I showed up at school. The children just stared at me, because they were the children of the workers of the C.F.E (*Comisión Federal de Electricidad*, Federal Electricity Commission).

There were also other students at the same school in town that were accustomed to being made fun of by the children of the C.F.E. employees. It was the only school in town and in some way they were right in thinking that they were the owners, because it had been built for them. But since there was no other, the C.F.E.'s union representative authorized the admission of all of the town's children. I am talking about the town, La Boquilla de Conchas, Chihuahua.

At the beginning, when they began to construct the dam, it was a C.F.E. encampment. It was priority for the federal government and they had to bring in people to build a hydroelectric plant. And so they build houses for their employees. And poor families that worked fishing and taking around tourists for a few pesos used that school. They took them around the lake (Lake Toronto) in boats. That is how these families supported themselves. Of course there were social and economic levels. The wives and children of the C.F.E. employees looked down on us and they were the upper class and never mingled with the poor.

Well, so when my parents arrived they had to look for work. My mama went to look for work with those people, asking for clothes to wash and iron for them. She didn't care what social class they belonged to. What she wanted was to help my papa so the family would progress.

And she also went directly to the school to enroll me. I was then 7 years old but I had attended a school on a *rancho* where my papa worked previously. His *patrón* was very conscientious. He ordered a large salon to be built where a teacher (female) gave classes to all the children of the *peons*. But the problem was we were all jumbled together and so we didn't learn much. In the school in La Boquilla it was easier because we were each in the grade we belonged to.

When my mama enrolled me in the first grade, the principal (female) said to her, "Look, *señora*, we are going to give your daughter a second grade exam. If she passes it, she will be in second grade, and if she doesn't, we will leave her in first grade. In any case you brought her to go into first grade, so there will be no problem." By then I knew how to read and write a little. My mama agreed. Then they gave me the exam and I passed it. And I was very content because I was going to be in a pretty school with many teachers and also many children.

But the sad reality was different. I didn't know that in the school there were class distinctions. And the first day that I attended I didn't know what row of children to line up with, because everyone lined up in the courtyard, and from there each grade went to their classrooms. Well, that day I remained standing at the door to the school. I didn't know what to do until the principal came by and said, "Come, we are going to take you to the classroom where you will be." And she took me and presented me to my teacher (male) and my classmates. Everything was very good, the children very courteous and the teacher as well. He gave me a welcome.

At this time I was very shy. I had never lived with other social classes of children. Always living on *ranchos*, I had no social contact with anyone, and besides, I was very sensitive. Well, I also stayed standing in the classroom, beside the desk, until the teacher told me, "Go and sit on the front bench with your little classmate." Well, I went timidly and with much embarrassment, sat down beside the girl: she was so well dressed. She was one of those from a higher class, and I with my humble dress and worn out shoes. However, my clothes and my shoes were very clean because my mama was thoughtful enough to bathe us every day. She heated water in a bucket over a fire and bathed us. She was very clean. If we didn't have bath soap, she bathed us with a bar of clothing soap. She bought creams and brilliantine by the gram, so that we would have them.

And so I went to school. I believed that the little girl was going to reject me for being poor and was surprised that she made friends with me. During recess she invited me to play. Since the school had a cooperative and the teachers sold candy, cookies, and all kind of sweets, she invited me to buy some and gave me all that she bought. But

13

the other children began to make fun of me, about how I was dressed. And the little girl defended me. Well, they began to change with her too, since she had become my little friend. Well, I felt fulfilled because I had someone to protect me. Because so it was that if anyone said something that bothered me, I would begin crying. For me it was an affront and a humiliation.

There was a boy much larger than I--he was in fourth grade while I was in second. He insulted me in front of the other children, and probably he was right about what he said. He had the custom of asking me my name, and before I could answer him saying, "Oh! I know your name is "you eat when you can," and he would begin laughing. And I of course began to weep silently because of pure sentiment and feelings of impotence, because I didn't know what to answer. I was very much a child. But then the teachers and the principal began to get to know me. Because my mother began to wash their clothing they had some consideration and affection for me. And if they heard they children laugh at me, they scolded them.

There was a classmate in my classroom who also defended me. And he told me, "I am going to take care of you and if they want to do something to you, tell me." He was a little older than me. He was 10 and I was 7. Well, from then on I had someone to protect me. And we grew up together, my little friend, him, and me. We always went around together.

Even though I had girl and boy cousins in school, I believe they were ashamed to say they were my relatives. But that didn't affect me. They were not close cousins. At this time I had only one first cousin. She indeed defended me and she was the one who helped me with my homework, explaining that it was because she was in fourth grade and I in second. I became very fond of her because she behaved very well toward me.

Time continued to pass and my father found work on a little *rancho* near La Boquilla, about 3 kilometers away. But I continued going to school. But now I stayed in my cousin's house. She was the daughter of one of my father's brothers. I stayed there from Monday through Friday, when my papa came for me.

At the beginning I went to the *rancho* every day at 5 in the afternoon upon getting out of school. But it was always dangerous, even though I didn't go alone. There were children who lived a little farther away than me. We were approximately six boys and girls, but we had to walk between the hills and down dirt roads. And I was a bit scared when we met up with pests, like scorpions, tarantulas, rattle snakes, and more, on the road.

When we arrived at the little house on the *rancho*, which was in the middle of the mountains, we lit our way with petroleum filled gaslights. I was panic-stricken about this place and even more so in the night when the coyotes howled. And I was even more afraid when we slept on the dirt floor on some thin mattresses my mama laid down for me and for my siblings. And at times my cousin came with me to spend the weekend with us. During the day it was very pretty because on the other side of the house there was a river and a little arroyo where we liked to go fishing.

There were times they did not pay my father at the end of his work-week and we had nothing to eat, and my cousin and I went to fish for mojarras. And we caught quite a lot. And my mother roasted them on the coals. And upon eating them, they were so tasty that why would we want anything else. Just with salsa and then to eat!

But I was happy. By then my mother had begun to acquire chicks, and raised the females to give eggs for me to go to town and vend. Meanwhile she went to wash the clothing of the rich ones and bring home a little corn and beans to give to my youngest siblings, until they paid my father his day's wages. He always worked in the fields as a day laborer. The *patrones* liked him a lot. Perhaps because he was a very hard worker or because—and not just because he is my father—he was always very honest and respectful.

I remember one weekend I arrived at my uncle's house so my papa would take me to the *rancho*, and my papa said to me, "Get ready what you are taking along, and I will come right back so we can go." I am talking about 6 in the evening, after having finished school. And I waited and he arrived for me about 8 at night, caring the few groceries that he was bringing home. It was only what the money his *patrón* paid him would buy. It was beans, corn, coffee for the pot, and sugar, a little of each, and oh!, some kilos of oranges for my siblings. Each one got half an orange.

Well the time came that he arrived to fetch me, and we left, I with tremendous fear, just knowing that we were going to walk and where panicked me. And he took my hand and off we went. There were times that there was no moonlight and I kept tripping over stones on the path. And there were times when it was very light. Well, I also was very afraid because under the moonlight the branches looked like snakes. And I was so frightened that upon arriving home my heart was out of place.

And my mama was waiting for us so she could cook the beans and corn to give my siblings dinner. At this time, about 10 at night, my mama and papa helped one another out, one to grind the uncooked beans with a mortar they had to grind *nixtamal* [corn flour for tortillas], so they would cook rapidly, and the other to cook corn to make tortillas in a little oven fueled by firewood that my papa had made for my mama. They made the dinner while my siblings slept. I remember my mama said to my papa, "As soon as the beans and tortillas are ready, I will wake up my children so they can eat, because I know the time to eat has passed, but not the day, and my children have to eat something and not sleep with their bellies filled only with air."

I was growing and getting older. When I was between 8 and 9 yeas old, I began to clean houses for the town's rich *señoras*. I didn't clean very well because there was furniture that I could not reach up far enough to clean. But I told the *señoras*, and they, very understandingly, said, "Don't worry, child. Just wash the dishes. The rest I will do. Just get ready to go to school so you won't be late."

They didn't give me much money, but they did pay me for washing the dishes for them, and sweeping and mopping the kitchen floors. A 50-cent coin that I thought was quite good. And furthermore, they collected clothing that they weren't using, and gave it to me. And well, afterward I went around more neatly, with well used clothing, but clean and well ironed.

I very much liked the work, because they fed me well, and they gave me money, or they bought me my school supplies. And so in this way I helped my parents to have one expense less. All this happened when we lived on the little *rancho* that I have mentioned in my narrative.

There were *señoras* who came to my uncle's and aunt's house to ask them if they would let me go to wash dishes, and they would buy my school supplies. And my aunt and uncle refused to give me permission. After time passed I understood that my aunt was right for not giving me permission because I could not go out unless my mama authorized it.

Afterward my father no longer had work because the harvest was scarce in the fields and the *patrón* died and his sons did not want to take charge of the lands. They were studying in Cuidad Juárez. And they had another way of thinking and the *rancho* was abandoned. And we had to migrate to the town once again. It was very difficult for my parents to begin anew in town because they could not find a house for relatively low rent or that someone would lend them, until a *señor* lent us two little rooms and we moved in.

I was very happy because I no longer had to walk to the *rancho* at night. And also, my mama didn't have to wait for my papa to arrive with the groceries, to give my siblings dinner at midnight. Nor did my mama have to take my younger siblings along when she went to wash other people's clothing. I took charge of them while she went to the houses to collect it and bring it home to wash. And I went to school and she waited for me to get out and help her to carry it. I got out at 1 p.m. to eat and entered at 3 p.m. and got out at 5 p.m. By then she had folded the clothes on the bank of the river, so I would go and deliver them.

At that time she charged 3 pesos for the dozen. She washed at least nine dozen pieces of clothing every day. That was another source of money and we ate a little better. And my father could not find a full time job. They employed him two or three days each week. And I felt very sad to see him so depressed--because he was used to working all week long from sunup to sundown. He came home very tired.

Well I arrived home after delivering the clothing my mama had washed, and set to making dinner with the little oven that served as a stove and that my father had made. I set myself to cooking beans and making coffee in the pot, so my father could eat--and to warming up the tortillas. Because I also had to make tortillas before I went to school. I had to get up at 5 in the morning to take the *nixtamal* for grinding, because there was an electric mill in town. I stopped grinding it in the mortar with which I had to mill the corn at least three times until it was ready to make tortillas.

I did not allow my mother to clean up after us. She also arrived very tired from being in the river washing clothes all day. It is also certain that they clothes the *señores* did not wear were given to my mama and she put patches on the pants that were torn to make them ready for my papa and my brothers. She was very good at patching pants. She sent the shoes that could hold up for three or four more times more of wearing for repairs, and then we wore almost new shoes. In one way or another we survived.

People now engaged my siblings to do errands for them, because now they were growing up. And they helped my papa with a little money, at least to pay for their school supplies. And I—to work in houses.

The situation was changing little by little. Now the school children did not make fun of me. The teachers accepted me as well. They esteemed me a lot. Some of them also brought me bags of used clothing. And I had many friends. The principal (female) put me to selling sweets at the school cooperative, and she said to me, "Ernestina, come to my desk. I want to talk to you." And she said to me, "You are going to vend and whatever sales you make, the money is for you, so that you can help your mother a little." And since I was very sensitive, my tears fell from emotion. But she warned me that this was going to be a secret so that the other girls did not get angry.

Time elapsed. Now I was in the 6th year of primary school, which cost me a lot of work because neither my papa nor my mama knew how to read or write. When I didn't understand something in the homework, I had to expend much effort to complete it. And they didn't let me go to the houses of classmates so they could help me. There were days that I lived with a very strong headache, whether because of the effort to learn or because of not eating well. But I always took my homework in. Almost always I got a grade of 8 [on a 10 point system].

This, yes, I was always number one in spelling. My teachers checked the notebooks. There were some classmates who were envious of me afterwards. They said I was an "ass-kisser." And I was not what they said I was. I just carried out my tasks. And in the classroom I behaved seriously. I didn't want them to send my mama any negative report, because I knew if I got one, she would take me out of school and send me to work in due form. And I didn't want this.

In fact, I was one year behind because my mama took me out of school to take care of my siblings while she went to work in the fields with my papa. I cried a lot but this didn't help me until the principal went to talk to her, to make her understand that the obligation to take care of the children was hers, not mine. But my mama, a little close-minded, answered that she was my mama, not her. And for the moment she was not going to send me to school but perhaps the following year, and I was not who was going to do what I wished. And there was no one who could make her understand. But I secretly sent my notebook to my teacher (female) so she would give me homework and grade it. And so I kept up. But since I was not on the list of those present in class, they did not validate this year. It was not until the next school year that I was able to go.

I entered 5th grade, and now everything was different. But I finished my primary school somewhat older, at age 14 and 6 months, almost 15. But I managed to finish. I very much wanted to continue studying, but our economic situation didn't allow me to. What I did was to leave school to find work in order to help my parents.

When I was scarcely 13 years old (1963), my papa had the opportunity to go as a *bracero* to Texas, and very well, we were not going to lack anything. But our pleasure endured only a short time. The contract ended and he returned, and back to the same thing, we suffering in poverty. But my mama had not been a fool. She had saved from the little money we received and with the savings she bought a little piece of land in La Boquilla and had a room built on it. And when my father returned we lived there, all of us piled up in the little room. But it was ours. Now it was different.

Afterwards another room was added, made of adobes that my papa manufactured. And *señores* who held us in esteem gave him materials so he could put on a roof. One *señor* who worked for the C.F.E. obtained wooden beams for him. And thus it was that we had our little house with two rooms. But we were very happy. And little by little my mama went along buying second-hand beds in installments. The same *señoras* that gave her clothing sold her furniture in exchange for having their clothes washed. But before that we slept on the floor on top of the clothing they gave her that no longer served for wearing. My mama made mattresses from the pant legs. She opened the seams and sewed the pant legs together in order to make a very wide bag. And what cloth was left over she put in the bag until a mattress was formed. And she also made sheets from the dresses that could no longer be used. But the thing is, now we didn't sleep on the floor, and we slept a little more comfortably, still all of us together, but warmer.

I felt very ashamed to see the conditions under which we lived. But everything was very clean. My mama was a person of very forceful character. I remember she put me to work washing dishes, all greasy and also sooty because she cooked with firewood. And at times there was no money to buy soap and I just looked at them and thought, how am I going to wash them without soap?

My mother was not capable of taking anything that did not belong to her. I am referring to the Clorox and soap that was left over when she washed clothing. She returned it all even if we didn't have any at home. And I didn't know how to wash the dishes. There were more than a few because we were thirteen in the family (we were four males and three females back then, and then another three females and three males came along, apart from the girl that my mother raised). She stood beside me and said, "Look, come along, I am going to show you how you can clean them." And she grabbed me by the hair and took me to where she cooked. She took a plate, took ashes out of the stove, and gave them to me. She said to me, "You are going to wash them with these ashes. And be careful that no grease or soot remains. And rinse them very well." She heated a little water to get rid of the grease, and then, with the ashes, they were clean. But beware if she saw a little spot of soot or a little grease! She piled them up again and made me wash them once more, until they were very clean.

It was very difficult to understand my mother and have to obey her, because there were beatings for whatever made her cross, and I was very sensitive. So it was to avoid her hitting me, I had to do whatever she ordered. And since I was the eldest, I had to be the example for obedience. My papa didn't interfere, he working from sunrise until the sun went down. The only thing he said when my mother complained about us, mostly about my siblings, was, "What do you want me to do? Kill them?" Because my siblings were terrible. They scarcely ever obeyed as she wished them to and she seldom ever hit them. But they made her very angry. And she took it out on me because I was the eldest. According to my mother I had to set an example.

It was a tough childhood for me. However, perhaps if my mother had not been so strict, who knows how we would have turned out? I don't say we were perfect children. But while my parents were alive, I was helping them out—even after I got married.

I remember when Christmas was nearing and I had many hopes and even more so when I heard the rich girls talking about what the Godchild (*niño díos*) was going to give them. And I, very innocent, wrote my little letter about what I wanted for my siblings. Then I went to cut a branch of mesquite and I decorated it with cotton that I brought back from a parcel of land. And I hung ornaments that I made from paper.

22

And it was my little Christmas tree. And then I put the little letter I had written to the Godchild in it.

Then it was Christmas Eve and I was unable to sleep, waiting for the Godchild to come with a bag of toys. And I never saw him enter. But how could he come in when my mama closed the door when we lay down! But I hoped he would knock. I was so naïve that I went outside to wait for him, hoping my mother would not find out, because she was a light sleeper who heard every little noise and got up to see what it was about.

The situation was very difficult for me. I knew that in the neighbors' houses they partied with *piñatas*, made their *buñuelos* [fried and sugared bread sticks traditionally eaten at Christmas time], their Christmas dinner, and we—nothing. But my mama made us believe she wasn't doing anything. I never saw her making *buñuelos*—not even this. The house was filled with sadness, but I didn't know it would disappear next day. And mama went out, and after a long while she returned with a closed cardboard box. And since she never permitted us to ask any questions, so it remained. The situation was that I was waiting sleeplessly to se when my and my siblings' toys would come--because I asked for model cars for my brothers, and a life size doll and a bicycle for me.

And from waiting so long I fell asleep until the following day. And the first thing I did was to go see my little tree. And what was my surprise, I found a box of *buñuelos* and for my little brothers little cars made out of metal. And for me thee was a rag doll that my mother had made. And she had hidden the presents in the house of an aunt so that we would not see them. And during the night she went and retrieved them and put them under the tree. I felt so disappointed and began to cry, saying to my mother, "That is not what I asked for." The letter even remained in the tree. And I, weeping, said, "Mama, he did not take my letter. Why not, if it was there that it was written what I requested?"

What my mama answered was, "This year he was very poor, and what do you want me to do? Be resigned to what he brought you. Besides, you all didn't behave very well. And give me that box. Let's see what is in it." And I gave it to her with tears in my eyes. And she opened it and said, "Look! It is *buñuelos*. Even this he brought you. I am going to make *atole* for you to drink."

I was happy because we had *buñuelos* and the corn *atoll*--without corn and without sugar--because the sugar had been use for the *buñuelos*, but it seemed very tasty. That day, the 25th, Christmas day, we all ate together. And my mama said to my papa, "Come and eat *buñuelos* and *atole* with your children. But you will be annoyed because there is no sugar." And since my papa liked to put a lot of sugar in his coffee, until it tasted like honey instead of coffee, he did not join us. Just looked out the corner of his eye at my mama and moaned and groaned. That is what he was accustomed to doing when he didn't like something. And he didn't like eating with us because he said he would eat after we all filled up, and he would eat what was left over. He said that he hassled himself working so that we had our bellies full and that he was satisfied with a taco.

But I know why he didn't eat with us. It was his strategy so my mama did not find out that he went to the store—he had his plans. And since my mama sent him to bring home corn and beans to cook, he brought a *bolillo* [a white roll with a hard crust] and a piece of sausage and a soda, and he consumed them happily. And I was a participant in this secret. It was the only way he could eat something he liked.

I thought it just since he worked so hard and couldn't eat what he liked. There were times he said to me, "Come along, my child. Let's go to the store so that you can take the corn to your nana rapidly." Because that it the word he used to say your mama or your mother. But now I knew what was happening. But one day my mother surprised him, and he became mute—with the bread almost to his mouth—when my mama said to him, "You like your treats!" The good thing is that I was not there at the time. If I had been she would have dragged me home by my hair.

My poor little papa had no choice but to buy another soda, for my mama. But her pride overcame her and it was enough for her to tell him to drink it himself, and that she would be waiting at home with the corn. Because now she knew why he spent so much time at the store. And my papa arrived with his tail between his legs believing that there was going to be a fight. And I was trembling with fear.

I thought she was going to say something to me as well. But nothing happened. My papa was waiting for her to scold him, but they only thing she asked him was, "Was the soda and bread good?" And my father just coughed. That was his custom when he didn't like something.

And my mama said to him, "I am in agreement, Antonio, that you have your pleasures. I know you have a right. But remember that I am waiting to cook the *nixtamal*--because you have me cooking at midnight. Come and leave it and then go to drink your little coca cola and eat your bread."

That was all she said. And I was so fearful. And it turned out that nothing more happened. In any case, it was me who waited for the corn for *nixtamal* to cook, and rinse it, and next day take it to the mill. I had to wait a long time for it to cool so that it could be rinsed. Or wait until the next day to get up early in the morning and rinse it. For me it was a routine. And it was not just one kilo or two. It was 5 kilos of corn besides that which was boiled. And that is what I took to be ground. But now I had the skills. I carried it on my head so the weight would not seem so heavy.

Perhaps some people, I do not know how many, who live in a country with extreme poverty, do not have to means to even put a taco in their mouths. But only he who suffers all this poverty knows what it really is--because we have lived through it. It's not just that you see it on the news, but also in our country there is a lot of extreme poverty. One should go to visit the indigenous communities where they even live in caves, enduring the inclement weather, and without being able to even raise a piece of tortilla to their mouths because of the lack of rain for their crops—which are principally corn and beans. Because not a drop of water falls and the earth is exhausted because of how dry it is. And there is no one to aid these poor families. And they do not dare to come down from their villages and ask for help, and even less so to go to the cities, because of the discrimination against them. And the government shines with its absence.

And they don't know or don't want to know that these poor families exist, and not even a census of them exists, because they have never been taken into account. But just like up in the mountains where they live, we have the same situation in the villages and in the very cities. Just because people do not have a permanent job, they do not take them into account because they are incidental workers. But the same government does nothing to resolve this problem so great in our country. And the populace still put up large signs saying, "Don't come to the city. There is no more room. Stay in your place of origin."

It is true there are many aid foundations—collection centers where all the help that can be left is gathered up--but this is done by good-hearted people who voluntarily contribute their little grain of sand. There are also foundations advertised on television. But all this comes from the citizenry, not the government. The poverty in the whole world is so great, not only in our country. On the news we see entire families dying of hunger.

I have mentioned to my children what I suffered as a child, together with their aunts and uncles and grandparents, but I believe that back then no matter how impoverished we were, we were rich. Because even though my father and my mother worked like burros, we had a piece of tortilla to put in our mouths. It is sad to say and apply this term (burros) to my parents, but they fact is they two sustained eight children while I was a child. Later the littlest ones were born, another three. I remember that back then the wages of a day laborer paid by the *patrón* were 10 pesos a day, and their daily expenses were between 20 and 25 pesos. My father was always indebted to the store that the same *patrón* owned in the village (La Boquilla). And what could he do? Well, continue working until the sun set, in order to pay off what he owed in installments—and he never finished paying.

I had great hopes to study and to work to pay for my schooling. But upon seeing the economic situation we suffered, all that was frustrated. The only thing I did was to go to work after I finished primary school. The good thing was that there was no need to search widely. Work came to me. My friend since second grade, and I thank her wherever she may be, found me work with an aunt of hers who lived in the nearest city to La Boquilla—Cuidad Camargo. It was a formal job. Back then I was 14 years and 5 months old, to be exact, and what I wanted was to work, even if it was as a servant. That didn't matter to me. I wanted my father to get out of debt because it was getting bigger and bigger, and my mama was always in the river washing clothes for others.

That *señora* contracted me to clean her house. It was not very big, but it was very dirty. When I began, everything went well, because she assigned me my work. She introduced me to her children. The eldest was exactly my age, but he looked like a bunny rabbit. The *señora* also, like my mother, had eight children, but with a great economic difference. Her husband, as I commented earlier, was secretary for the C.F.E. He was very nice, and the *señora* a bit of a despot. But it didn't concern me. I went to work, period. They paid me 120 pesos a month, because at that time it was the going rate. I was very content when I received my first wages. I immediately took them to my mama, and she was very happy. I only gave her 25 pesos, because I had to keep back 5 pesos each week for the bus. [Ernestina was paid every two weeks, so received 60 pesos for her first wages].

And since I liked to go walking in the plaza, I invited my friend and she and I ate an ice cream and talked to the boys for a while. And then we returned home. My mama now let me go out without any pretext. And since she knew that now I followed a pattern of obedience and discipline, she had no problems with me.

And so I stayed working with this family for almost two years. Well, now it was not just cleaning the house: little by little she had me enter the kitchen work. First she asked me to make flour tortillas, and I, very obedient, made them while she prepared the dinner. But later she wanted more, make tortillas and make dinner. Now she did not ask me the favor of helping her. Now it was part of my work. And to keep my work, I did it. And if I didn't do it, she got angry. Well, that was not enough for her, and the *señora* had me do everything, because she went out with her woman friends and took a long time in returning. And I, well, screw you, Ernestina.

And to take care of the many kids she had was the same as in my own house, with the difference being that with her I got a salary. And because of this, I contained myself. And furthermore, her children treated me very well. We had no quarrels. Nor with the *señor*—he was very nice. He did not put on any airs. Because of this, I endured. He came home from work and if he found making dinner and making tortillas, he did not mind—he served himself. I really liked that he did so, because it made me feel he trusted me.

One among many days that I was making dinner, he asked me, "What are you making for dinner today?" And it occurred to me to answer him, "chiriguais"--a word I invented--with potatoes. I didn't even know what it was that I answered. And he began laughing and said, "Well serve me a large plate of them. Let's see what it tastes like."

And I served him and I knew what I had cooked. It was sausages with potatoes and mashed beans with red chili sauce seasoned with a bit of oregano. And from that time on, he called me "chiriguais." And he called me that all the time. And I never felt badly about it. On the contrary, I felt that he said it with affection. But one day his wife asked him why he called me that and he answered her that he liked to, and period.

At times I felt uncomfortable, not with the *señor* but with the *señora*—that she might get annoyed with me. But that was the *señor*'s character. He had no quarrel with anyone. All of their children treated me as though I was one of the family. And since almost all of their relatives were from La Boquilla, they knew me and knew who my parents were, and they esteemed me.

But the *señora* was quarrelsome. There were even two times she accused me of being a thief. According to her she had lost a watch. And she went to check my suitcase (I call it a suitcase, but it was just a miserable cardboard box). And she found nothing. And she was saying to me that I should give it back to her. That she had never lost anything until I came to work. Well, I, completely fearful, swore that I had not taken it and if she wished I would help her look for it in her bedroom. Or that she ask her girls if they had taken it. And she said, "I don't believe so, because they never take anything of mine."

The truth is that I was frightened. But I began thinking, she is doing this so I quit and she doesn't have to pay me, but why doesn't she say outright that she doesn't want my services anymore? And if I leave she is going to say that I indeed stole from her. And I didn't know what to think. I was at a crossroads. The only thing I did was to go to my room and cry and ask God that she find it and not blame me for something I hadn't done.

Well, this moment passed. The children arrived from school. And since I slept in the same room as the girls, one of them found me there, sobbing. She embraced me and asked me what had happened. And I told her. And she answered me, "Ay, my mama. For sure she does not remember that she gave it to me so that I would keep it while we went to La Boquilla pools, since she was going to go in to swim. I have put it away. Come on. We are going to give it back to her. And I apologize."

I didn't want to go with her because I felt very badly—no one had ever accused me of being a thief. And from that day on I did not feel comfortable there. The *señora* came and asked me to forgive her, that she had not remembered this detail. That she was very sorry but I too would perhaps have thought the same. Perhaps she was right. If there is a stranger in the house it is logical to think or believe this.

Many things happened during my stay in this house, but in order to keep the work I so needed, I endured a lot. And then I was like the little pitcher from Guadalajara that with any little tap broke into pieces. I have heard this said when a person is very sensitive.

I never told my mama what had happened, because I knew how she would react. Better to remain silent. But there was another occasion that I could not endure. I packed up my goats and returned to La Boquilla. Well, she accused me of having stolen a sock from one of her children. And then she went and took it out of my suitcase, and said to me, "I didn't find the watch in the suitcase, but I did find the sock, and with reason I blamed you." She said to me, "Here is the evidence."

I felt like the worst thief in the world. I felt like I was going to faint, I didn't know whether from anger or from shame. But I reacted quickly and said to her, "Look, *señora*, if you no longer want me to work with you, just tell me and I will go. There is no need to try to entrap me. Because, up until now, hear me, no one has ever accused anyone in my family of being thieves. We have many needs but we have never stolen anything and even less so a measly sock. And I am absolutely certain that it was you who hid it in my suitcase. But I am going to give you the pleasure of seeing me go. And be careful that it does not reach my mother's ears, because she will see that you eat your words." Because my mother becomes like a wild beast when it comes to defending her children.

And so it was that I stopped working for this family. When I arrived home my mother was surprised, because she saw me coming with my supposed suitcase. And I felt among the unhappiest people in the world. I didn't want to know anything. The good thing was that one of the *señora*'s sisters-in-law lived in front of her house, and I asked her to lend me money to pay for the bus. Her sister-in-law knew what kind of sister-in-law she had. And she said to me, "It seemed strange to me that she did not run you off sooner, because she has run off many workers, so as not to pay them. Well, I am very sorry because I was wanting you for my brother who is very much in love with you. I am going to tell him to go and visit you in La Boquilla."

"Tell him that whenever he wants to come, I will be in La Boquilla." But I didn't want to talk a lot. "Are you going to lend me money for the bus?"

"Of course I will lend it to you. How much do you want?"

"Just enough to get to La Boquilla--two and a half pesos. I'll pay you back when your sister-in-law goes to my house to pay me."

"You believe she will go?"

"If she has any shame she will go. But don't worry. Send it to me with your brother."

"Really?

"Send it with him."

"He is going to be very happy that you left that house. Because of that he didn't even want to stop by. But now that you will be in La Boquilla, he is going to be eager to see you. As soon as the weekend comes he will go to visit you, and for me, poor you if you reject him."

"No, how can you believe that, if for me the week will stretch out while I wait for him?"

I felt very sorry about leaving this house because I was very fond of the children. I was most sorry about the littlest children, because if I did not put them to sleep, they did not sleep, and the *señora* left everything to me. But well, I went along with the idea that I would have to forget them.

And the saddest thing is that when I arrived at my house, I didn't bring a cent. And because I came home with all my clothes, my mother asked me what had happened with my job. I didn't want to tell her anything, but it was necessary to tell her a compassionate lie. I told her I was very tired because I had been left to do all the work, and it was very hard for me. And what she said to me was, "You should have waited until the end of the month and she paid you."

"No mama, the *señora* Margarita is very demanding." That was her name. By now she is certainly deceased.

Later I went to retrieve the money owed me, because it wasn't fair that she kept back part of my salary. And what she did was to tell me, "I am not going to pay you. I personally am going to take it to your mama. I want to talk to her."

And the first thing that I thought was that this *señora* wanted to go and gossip about everything with my mama. But she didn't know whom she was going to confront. "Well, go ahead. I am not worried about it."

But I did worry about how my mother was going to react. She didn't see what someone does to her, but how someone pays her. Because it was not the first time my mother fought with someone. I was very ashamed that she went about fighting. But she was right. She said, "They can do to me whatever they wish, but don't touch a hair of my children." And that was the reason I was afraid the *señora* would come.

Well, I returned and told my mama that the *señora* was going to come and pay her, that she didn't want to pay me. "Well then, I'll wait to see what she has to tell me. For certain it is some gossip about you. That's why she didn't want to pay you. And if she comes I want you to be here with me, to see what gossip she brings." And since I hadn't told her the truth about why I left the job so suddenly, she didn't believe me.

Everything was fine. The rest of the week I went with my mama to help her rinse the clothing in the river, while she washed the rest of it. She said nothing to me, but when Saturday arrived, my ex-*patrona* arrived as if nothing had happened, saying that I had left without giving her notice, and that she was bringing my monthly wages. She gave my mama the whole months wages, even though I had not worked the full month. And my mother accepted them. She asked my mama's permission to let me work again. And my mother turned to me as if to say, "You know if you want to go." And I making signs that I did not want to. But it was she who decided. The *señora* said to my mama that if she gave me permission she would pass by for me in the afternoon.

I didn't want to say anything. I prepared myself and went along, not very happily. But I decided that if she accused me of being a thief again, I was not going to take it, and I would tell my mother everything. It was a very uncomfortable situation for me. But I had to endure it. I pretended that nothing had happened and waited to hear what the *señora* would say to me.

And when we arrived at her house she called me to her room and asked forgiveness. And she said that she herself had hidden the sock among my clothing, because she couldn't find a way to recover from what had happened with the famous watch that her daughter was keeping for her, and that it made her feel ashamed. The situation was that she never blamed me for anything again. I didn't know whether it weighed on her conscience or whether someone had sent for me. I didn't want to investigate.

Afterwards she behaved very nicely towards me. She didn't make me work so much. Now when she went to visit her friends she told me she would be back early. Now she was not so demanding--but now I knew what I had to do. Everything was very different. And when the whole family went out for a stroll they took me along to have a good time with them. Now I trusted her more, enough to ask her permission to go to a commercial school that was free. One only had to buy the necessary materials. It seemed good to her.

In this school they taught social etiquette, baking, dressmaking, painting, drawing, and embroidery. But my pleasure did not last long. I was investing too much, and it was little that I was contributing to my family. Well, I had to leave. I was there about seven months. And during this time I took almost nothing home, apart from the fact that I had to buy my personal things. I couldn't do it all. Even though they gave me a raise of 5 pesos a week, it wasn't sufficient for my expenses. I left aside these 5 pesos for my bus ride and gave 30 pesos to my mama.

But what worried me most was the eternal debt with the store. And I said to my papa that it was a famous *tienda de raya* (company store), like in the past times—before the Revolution. The *patrón* kept them constantly indebted in order to oblige them to work for him and pay them a starvation wage. Because my papa's employer was the store-owner. Because of this my papa always worked for the same *patrón*. Almost since the time when we first arrived in La Boquilla, my father is who carried out all the work, tilling the earth with a plow and a mule to prepare the soil for sowing. When the season came for that which had been planted to come up, he watered it. He spent days watering. At times we even had to bring him dinner because he could not leave the water on, because the trenches would overflow.

At times my papa sowed cotton, other times corn and peanuts, even tomatoes and chili. And so it was variable. I am not talking about just one or two hectares. It was almost twenty. Apart from this he planted seven hectares of walnuts the he also had to water, so they did not dry up. Whether it was summer of winter he had to go into the water, because this land was irrigated.

I saw my father arriving very tired and unable to sleep, his legs torn up from being in the mud and water, all cracked open. And my mama had to prepare a bucket of hot water for him, so he could soak his legs and cure them, because no one wore rubber boots--just sandals that he himself made, with a sole from a car tire, and straps of leather. But such was his work. Because of this nobody wanted to work for the *señor*.

The work in the fields was very hard for my father. He had no one to help him. This is what motivated me to look for work and try to help them. I remember when my mother heated water so he could put his legs in it. They were all dried up from mud and water. And when he was washing his legs, my mama was watching to see how they were and said "Antonio, there are not cracks, they are canyons! I am going to have to cover all these cracks with a pomade that I am going to make. But you have to use it ever day, as soon as you return from work." Afterwards, he did not bleed from the dryness.

My mama went to get candles and petroleum oil, that back then were easy to acquire, and heated the paraffin from the candles until it became liquid. Afterwards she added the oil. She stirred it until it formed a pomade and smeared it on the cracks. She filled them with this pomade and wrapped each of his legs with a cloth. My papa just moaned when she rubbed his heals, because it was his heels where there were most cracks, and most deep.

My poor little papa: I remember him and it comes to mind how I saw him groaning. But my mama didn't say anything until she saw him limping, and she asked him why he was walking that way. And he said, in his own way, "Well, who knows. I have pain in my paws and my legs." And that was when my mama found out what was bothering him. But with her miraculous pomade, the famous canyons, as she called them were healed. And then later he himself asked her to bring it to the fields so he could put it one when he got out of the irrigation ditches. He did not even dare to ask the *patrón* for some rubber boots for when he was watering the crops.

The only thing that interested the *patrón* was that his lands were producing. My mama, in spite of her stern character, was very understanding with my papa, and she often told him to leave this job. And my papa answered her, "With what in the heck are we going to pay what we owe to this *señor*?"

"Well, we will see with what."

The good thing was that my younger siblings began to grow up and they offered themselves to do errands for the *señoras*. Well, they earned their tips, and took the change to my mama, and she saved it so they could buy their notebooks or whatever they needed for school. That was one less expense for her.

The salary that the *señora* Margarita paid me was not sufficient. Now it was necessary for me to look for another job where they paid me more. But with the little schooling I had, I didn't know how to do anything else but clean houses, and could not aspire to do anything else. After all the problems went away, I was happy where I was working. And over all, I was beginning to like boys and I had to be better dressed and look for someone I liked and who liked me.

Well, just as I wished, my prince charming appeared. I looked at him and liked him, and he looked back at me. He invited me to take a walk around the village plaza. I accepted and said to myself, "This one is going to be mine." Well, that is the way it went. We spent some days going out as friends. He was not from La Boquilla, but from Cuidad Camargo. But since he had an uncle in La Boquilla, he slept there.

He had already seen me before, when passing by the house where I worked, but I had not even noticed him. But he had noticed me and said that he hadn't dared to talk to me because he believed I was very quick tempered since he saw me as being very serious. And then he asked me if I would like to be his sweetheart. And I answered yes, with one condition, that he go and speak to my parents, because I didn't want to go out with him secretly or leave the house without permission. And my parents, in order that we not meet secretly, did give permission.

He treated me very seriously despite the fact that he was very young back then—19-years-old. But I liked his personality. We always went around hand-in-hand.

When we sat on a bench in the plaza, he put his arm around my shoulders as if he wanted to embrace me but didn't dare. Our relationship was very lovely.

When he went to play basketball he took me along so I could see him play. He participated at both state and municipal level. He also was a relay runner in the 20-kilometer races held when the annual festival of the patron saint, the Virgin of Perpetual Aid, was celebrated in Camargo. His whole family was very Catholic, and during that time, I let myself be led by them. We were at mass at the earliest hour on Sunday and when I got out I took the bus to La Boquilla. And in my house almost no one had the custom of attending church.

The only one who was devout was my papa. He even had an emblem of the adorers of Christ. But only he went to the Catholic Church. My mama had no religion and she said that there was no need to go to church in order to be in good with God and that her only religion was to go the river and screw herself washing clothing--that that was her religion and her penitence.

My mother was a bit negative about religion, but the strange thing was, when one of my little brothers got sick when he was a child, she went to the Church. And she said to my papa that she had dedicated him to the Santo Niño de Atocha, who was supposedly very miraculous, and if he got better she would dress him like that said. My brother got better. And my poor little brother was about three years old and went around dressed like the Santo Niño de Atocha.

My mother always had a presentment about something, but didn't know if it was about my papa or simply about the so precarious situation that we always found ourselves in. And even so, my uncle by marriage went and left her a 40-day-old baby girl, who she raised along with my recently born little brother. There is only a week's difference in age between them.

According to my uncle she was to stay with us for only 6 months, and he would help out with the milk and the cloth for diapers. He came to say that he was leaving the baby girl because my aunt, my mother's sister, had died giving birth, and the other children had left, and their eldest little girl had been taken away by her grandmother. I scarcely remember what happened but as soon as my uncle left my mother began crying for the loss of her sister and upon seeing this so helpless little girl.

My mama said to me when I saw my sister—and I say my sister because in the final analysis she grew up with us (I was barely 5 years old when she arrived)—"I wonder what kind of future awaits her with us if I scarcely have enough milk for my little boy? Well, anyway, I am going to share my milk with both of them. And look, daughter, how she grabs my breast as though she were starving."

I mention all this because one speech or one narration leads to another, and if I am narrating or entering into a dialogue, that is what I am doing. Perhaps it seems fantasy-like or a little exaggerated, but these things were happening. My brother, the one I am referring to, was very dominating from childhood on. And my mama let him do anything he liked in the house, and my papa ignored him, because he didn't even let my brother who comes after me control him. He grew up resenting the little girl. And when I got work in Mexico City, I separated myself from them.

Even though I had a boyfriend, it didn't matter. When my boyfriend saw that I was going to leave to work in Mexico City, he proposed to me. But back then I had no thoughts of marriage. I was very young. According to me, I was not going to marry until I was 18 or 21 years old.

A *señora* from Camargo, married to a man who was the owner of a window blind and curtain rod factory in Mexico City, asked my mother permission to take me to work in their house there. And my mama let me go. The *señor*, together with his

brothers, was also the owner of a fishing cooperative and an ice-making factory in the

town. They were the richest family in La Boquilla, and descendants of Spaniards. They

also owned the movie theater in town. But they were very good people.

So I left my entire family, my sweetheart, my friends, and the town where I

grew up. Even though my sweetheart and I wrote back and forth a lot, it was not the

same. My sweetheart and I saw each other when my *patrón*'s children were on school

vacations--when the family returned to La Boquilla.

Supposedly they had hired me as a cook, without my knowing what food I was

to make for them, since I didn't know anything about their meals. But I didn't have

many problems, because the *señora* let me know what they wanted and how to make it.

It was not complicated food. I learned fast. And she would ask me, "Tina, what are

you going to make for us to eat today?"

And I replied, "Whatever you like."

And it occurred to me to make a creamed pea dish to begin, a noodle soup, beef

steak stewed in green chili sauce, and for desert, jello. All this seemed easy enough to

prepare. There were times when I ran out of ideas and didn't know what to cook. Well,

I had to invent some meal or another. The good thing is that neither they nor their

children were fussy about what they ate. There were times that the *patrón* asked to be

sent boxes of fish in ice from La Boquilla, and then they had much variety in their

meals.

At times, nothing seemed real, because in Camargo I supposedly worked as a

house cleaner and suddenly I found myself in the kitchen, because they had a girl who

cleaned and took care of the children for them. It was not just one or two children, but

five—four girls and a boy—between two and ten years old.

And from earning 120 pesos a month to earning 200 pesos a month, well, it seemed very good to me, but I was far away from everyone. My first month's wages arrived and I got my money, but I did not know how to send it to my family. And I had to ask the girl who worked there how to do it. She took me to the post office and told me what to do. That it was easiest and fastest via telegram. That the post office was going to give me a receipt showing the amount I sent. That my mother would receive a notice from the telegraph office so she could go and claim it. And later I asked my employer if when he passed by the post office, could he send it for me? And he did so. He just handed over the receipt to me. And he would come home and say to me, "Now I have sent the money to your mama. Here's the voucher." As I said, they were good people.

And every time they went on a trip, sometimes to Cuernavaca, they took us along in the station wagon they owned, and not just to take care of the children. It was also for our entertainment. They made us feel part of the family. And since I have always liked soccer, the *patrón* took me to the Estado Azteca [the main sports stadium in Mexico City] to see the games, along with the mean and women who worked for the factory.

The *señora* gave me a little money to buy yarn to crochet with, and to buy a little clothing, because she knew that I was left with no money since I sent it to my family. She didn't give me a very lot, but I tried to make the money stretch and I went to a clothing store where the clothes were cheap and very pretty. The owner of the store was an actor called Raúl Astor, and he had a chain of stores called "Tiendas Astor."

And later on I knew to reach the main square in Mexico City, called the Zócalo, by myself. Back then one could still walk around without any danger of being assaulted by anyone. Of course if you went into some neighborhoods, like the barrio of Tepito,

La Candelaria de los Patos, La Colonia Diez de Mayo, for example, it was dangerous, because they assaulted and even killed people.

I walked around the Zócalo very happily, because the bus stopped there, and from there you could get another bus back to the factory, where the house also was. My *patrones* lived in what was a famous *colonia* that continues to be famous—Colonia Alfonso XIII—near the northern periphery (*periférico norte*).

Everything was very different now. I was living in another stage in my life. But my feet still hadn't left the soil of my place of origin. My *patrón*'s brother-in-law also had stock in the window blind and curtain rod company, and he was also from Cuidad Camargo. He engaged me to clean his office. It was some extra money. But I kept this money back. It wasn't millions, but it was enough so I could buy some sweets occasionally. And I was happy in this house. My anxieties were lessened by knowing that all of the little bit of money I earned reached my parents.

Ernestina and her mother in Baja California

Ernestina's father in Baja California

Chapter 2. From Mexico City to Mexicali

Afterwards, time passed. About 3 or 4 months later I met the man who would become my husband. I met Adolfo. He was one of the trusted employees of the business of which my *patrón* was the owner. Well, Adolfo came to look for the *patrón* and there he met me and introduced himself. And while I took care of my *patrón* who was also his *patrón*, we began talking. And since I didn't have the least idea of having a boyfriend in Mexico City, I approached it as a friendship. But from this day on he began to court me. And I rejected him. But he persisted, and began bringing me chocolates every day. He thought that by doing so he would win me over.

Well, it lasted like that for about a year. We did go out to the movie theater and he took me to his parent's house. They received me nicely. But he introduced me as his sweetheart and that did not seem proper to me because we were nothing more than friends. On weekends he got drunk and shouted at me from the sidewalk. And I felt ashamed in front of my *patrones* because of the scandal he was causing. And I had to go out and tell him to go away and that he had no right to be shouting at me, that we were not engaged. And he kept on being insistent that he wanted us to be engaged.

Until one day, while sober, Adolfo spoke to me courteously and said that he wanted us to be sweethearts. He promised me he would no longer drink. I asked him to give me time. And so we became sweethearts. I cut off my relationship with my boyfriend in Camargo and became Adolfo's girlfriend. Everything went along well. He stopped drinking. I went along quite happy with him, but then he began to get jealous of me for whatever thing I did. He did not let me talk to any male friend. If he took me out to dine, he didn't want me to look at any man, because, Adolfo said, that the man would want me to go with him. I don't know if he did it on purpose to bother me or whether he was indeed jealous. Almost always when I went out with Adolfo I had to

44

walk with my glance straight ahead or looking at the ground. And it was frustrating for me. He was very possessive. That was my life as his sweetheart. We married with me believing he would change. But it became worse. I will speak more about this later.

[Ernestina had one child each year for 8 years after marrying Adolfo, usually becoming pregnant against her will. While in Mexico City she earned money making and repairing clothes with a sewing machine she had at home. She continues to do this in Mexicali.]

When we decided to go to Rosarito, B.C., it was so I could be reunited with my parents. Well, I don't remember very well how and when my parents came to Rosarito because I was married and living in the Federal District at the time, but according to one of my sisters it seems my papa migrated first. It was in the 1970s. And later he sent for the whole family. It is that everyone migrates to the border to search for work because in their birthplace work is scarce and they have to look for other horizons. And in this case, it fell to my father to migrate to Rosarito.

My papa bought a house lot that the *ejido* commissioner made easy for him to pay off. And my mama paid for a room to be made of wood, with the money from the things she had sold in Chihuahua, where we are from. And she put a down payment on it and also paid for the rest in installments. They both died in Rosarito.

The house they had bought, or better, the room where they lived, burned down. The municipal government gave them materials so they could rebuild. My siblings immediately went about raising the walls. And my papa and my younger siblings—by then they had grown up—began to sell ice cream bars on the beach in order to bring a little money into the house, but for sure, without stopping going to school. Because poor as they were, my mother never stopped sending us to school.

What also happened was that the delegate from Rosarito promised my mama that he would help her go to Chihuahua to retrieve copies of her personal documents, that had burned in the fire. Well with much commotion or uproar, the house where the whole family got together when we went to visit them, was built. But after having had 11 children, they were alone. And my mama began to get ill when they found out they would have to leave the house because one of my brothers, though deception, had sold it without the rest of us knowing. We found out that they had been thrown out of the house and taken to an *ejido* where one of my sisters lived, with the promise of building them a house on this *ejido*. And they never saw either the money from the sale, or the famous house that was to be built.

And as a consequence of this my mama became sad and started to have mental gaps. She began having a lot of pain in her gall bladder, until they operated on her. She did not last more than two months after the operation, and died in 2008. From the moment of my mother's death, my father began to decline—to the degree that he did not want to eat anymore. We had to force him to eat. It got so bad that my niece, she who had been taking care of both of them, telephoned me all the time, saying that her papa Toño—because that is what all his grandchildren called him—didn't want to eat and every once in a while he fainted because he was so weak. That at all hours of night they had to take him to the hospital and she didn't have the money to pay for his care, except what my sisters María and Elizabeth and I gave her. But she found a way to take him for treatment. All of us sisters worked at this time and couldn't be with him.

My only option was to move him to Mexicali, to where we had relocated, so that one of my sons could take care of him. At that time my son was not working and that made it easy for him. We took care of him while it was not hot in Mexicali. Everything went well, buying his vitamins, making him his little soups. And my workmates discovered my situation and began helping me economically by giving me their food stamps. One of them brought me boxes full of Ensure. As I said, everything went well. But when it began to get hot my sisters took him to Rosarito, because he could not stand the heat, and even less so in the condition he was in. But he only lasted 3 months and then died of a heart attack.

He had no will to live. We would talk after I got home from work and he said he wanted to die because he was a burden to us. And every once in awhile he remembered his little old lady, and tears fell. They had been married 63 years. How would he not miss her? With and without problems they got ahead—my mother with her overwhelming personality and he who was so passive that he put up with everything. But it is true that no one worked harder than they did. They were burros, in the good sense of the word.

I don't want to remember any more now because I become overcome with nostalgia and my heart becomes tied up in knots. I know they are with us. Wherever they are, they send us their blessings. I love them: even though they are not here physically, they are her spiritually. And I hope that my brother—with his dirty trick of dispossessing them of their house—one day repents and asks God's pardon for the harm he did them. Because he didn't even contribute for my father's funeral.

May God forgive you, brother!

We lived almost a year in the same house with my parents. Thereafter we moved to our land that Adolfo had bought with the help of the *ejido* commissioner in one of the largest colonias in Rosarito. It's name was Colonia Ejido Mazatán. Adolfo did not have stable work. After an accident he had while working for Pemex he worked as a sales agent for encyclopedias. It was intermittent work with Pemex, but the good thing was that Pemex gave him Social Security when he had an accident. After about two years in which he was going for therapy, they gave him a disability pension. He could no longer do heavy work or lift heavy things. And he continued working, but as a sales agent selling encyclopedias. There were days when he made no sale and came home tired from so much walking, up and down streets, from house to house, without selling anything. But there were times that it went well for him, because he made three or four sales. And then we had enough to feed the eight small children we then had.

But it didn't always go well for him, even though my parents helped us a lot. For this I thank them and appreciate them, and even less forget them. But we could not always be relying on them to help out.

Well, Adolfo left this work because he had to take the bus from Rosarito to Tijuana, where his work was, and this was a heavy expense. The circumstance was that he left this job and I had to look for work cleaning houses in a tourist center to support him and the children and so that Adolfo could continue going to therapy. The tourist center is called San Antonio del Mar, if they have not changed its name by now.

All of this that I am writing about happened between 1978 and the end of 1981, when we moved to Tijuana and then went on to Mexicali at the end of 1981, and up until today.

I was 6 months pregnant with my son Gustavo when we moved to the Colonia Ejido Mazatlán. Adolfo arrived from work and before he ate dinner he invited me to go for a walk. And he took me to a place where there were no houses and he said to me, "Let's rest awhile and then we will continue walking." And I, very obedient, stopped to rest. But it was not for this reason we stopped. He remained standing, looking about in all directions, then began beating me in my stomach with his closed fist. And I did not know what motive he had for doing it. He didn't say anything to me. And I only struggled with the pain I had and only tears fell from my eyes and I felt as though my child had moved inside me. Adolfo didn't even give me the opportunity to ask him what I had done to make him beat me in this way. The only thing he did was to clean away my tears for our return home so that my parents would not suspect anything-- because we were living with them until we moved to our little plot of land that we had bought. They never knew what Adolfo did to me because I didn't want to involve them, so that there would not be problems.

On another occasion, when I began to work at the tourist encampment, he also brought a lawsuit against me for an imagined adultery, and this time my brother Isidro and my mama were involved. But since there was no proof the judge dismissed the case. My mama, believing Adolfo, threw me out of the house and I had to take refuge with a *señora* until Adolfo talked me into returning, that I do so for my children, and that no one else but me could take good care of them. I accepted on the condition that we would leave Rosarito. We sold the house to one of my brothers, and with the money we bought one in Tijuana.

I believed everything would change. But Adolfo remained the same. There were more problems and it became worse. Since the court did not proceed with the accusation he made, he felt like a loser. Now, far from my family, he did what he wanted to me. He beat me all over my body, he kicked me until I fainted. And he put the television on the highest volume so that my children would not hear what he was doing to me. He even hit me in my face with his closed fist, leaving me with blackened eyes, accusing me of having a lover and asking me where we had agreed to meet in order to go to a hotel.

I stood all this, but simply because I didn't want my children to one day reproach me for leaving them without a father, or simply because of my foolish belief that one married for life. We spent about a year in Tijuana and then went on to Mexicali. And we left the godparents of my son Toño's school graduation in charge of the house. Later we found out that they had placed some relatives of theirs in the house, and they kept all our possessions. Adolfo didn't want to go to throw them out.

And my children never knew what their papa did to me, or they said nothing about it because they were afraid. They knew what a womanizer he was but they never said anything to me about the way he mistreated me. Nor have I said anything to them about it. This was my life in Rosarito and Tijuana. I don't want to tell anything more because I get emotional and begin crying from anger and pain. In spite of everything that happened to me with this man—or whatever you wish to call him—may all go well with him and this woman he went away with. I do not wish him ill, and good or bad, my offspring are his offspring. If he ever comes to visit them, that is their problems.

I do not want to remember everything because it fills me with nostalgia and at the same time the anger defeats me. And I would like to see Adolfo and tell him that one day he will die, and when I saw him and he greeted me, I didn't recognize him. But we never have come face-to-face to argue, because he does not lend himself to a conversation. He is and always has been very *machista*.

In October of 1981 we arrived in Mexicali on our way back to Mexico City. We went to visit my mother's sister ad her family with the pretext of greeting them [which among relatives would mean they would be offered lodging]. But in reality we wanted to stay there while Adolfo asked for his resignation from the maquiladora where he worked in Tijuana. And he left the whole family with them and did not resign. By now, two months had passed and I did not see anything about his resignation and the money we had brought had been spent. And my uncle and my cousins did not want us to be there in their house and the children were not able to go to school. I had to look for a house to rent and when Adolfo arrived I told him that they were running us off. But he brought the money from his resignation [severance pay].

But now he did not want to go to Mexico City, to where we were going to return from Tijuana. And so we obtained a house that someone lent us, that didn't have running water or electricity. And we had to enroll our children in school. And with the money he brought, a part we spent on school supplies and that which was left we spent on food. We also had to buy a gasoline stove to cook on. And so we made count what was left over, at that time 260 *pesos*. And because of the commentary of a *señor* we went to sell newspapers.

And Adolfo asked if I would be willing to sell newspapers. And I told him, yes, but with whom were the children going to stay? And he answered me that we could change their schedule so that they went to school in the afternoon while we sold newspapers. They entered school in the afternoon and we took with us the two youngest, Guillermo and Gustavo. And the plan seemed good to me, so that is what we did.

And when we went to the press (*Centinela*, an afternoon newspaper), we took the money that I mentioned, 260 *pesos*, and we wanted to exchange all the money for newspapers. But with good luck, the man in charge of the newspaper told us "If you are willing to sell, I am going to give you 100 newspapers. And if you decide to continue vending, I will wait for you tomorrow and I will set aside another 100. But these are going to be charged for after you sell them. Are you in agreement?"

"Yes, *señor*. Here we go."

"Well, good luck." And we left immediately.

Well, 100 newspapers seemed few to us and we went home very happy. With the money we earned we went to the Calimax supermarket that was at this time on the corner of Justo Sierra and Calzada Aviación. We were living in Colonia Miraflores. We bought our children a gallon of milk and something to eat for dinner. And it broke my heart to see my children, who had had almost all the comforts—though not luxuries--sleep on the old mattresses, all stained, that we had bought for them. I didn't know if the stains were from urine or from the rain. And some sheets that a cousin by marriage gave us.

I have much to thank her for because she was who helped us, giving us plates and a pot to cook beans in. I will not omit her name—Esther. I don't remember her surname but I know that Zapata is the name of my cousin--Esther's husband. And my children liked her a lot. They still today have much respect for her. And principally Magali liked her a lot because she took her to the *tianguis* [weekly market] and bought her clothing.

And this is when we began to sell newspapers. Later, even though we stayed in the same house, we were buying second-hand furniture—we were better off.

Chapter 3. Life in Colonia Miraflores

It was advisable for us to get along with our neighbors when we lived in Colonia Miraflores--because they would take care of my children. Of course there were drug addicts who when they were taking drugs didn't recognize people, but now we knew who they were and we just greeted them. There was one occasion when a boy went a hid a knife in the fence surround the house. And I noticed that he had hidden something and when he left I went to see what he had put there. And when I saw it was a knife I picked it up, because it represented a danger to my children--that they might see it and take it. But the following day he came by and asked me about what he had left in the fence, and I told him that I had taken a knife that was hidden there. And he told me that was what he was looking for. He asked if I could give it back to him. And I told him that he should not be leaving anything because my children might find out and I was not going to be responsible if he lost whatever he left. And they never left anything again.

To tell the truth I was not very happy in that *colonia*, and even less on the street where we lived, even though they didn't do anything to us. But the mere fact of living there made me frightened for my children.

It also happened that I saw a woman murdered in the street. She had been stabbed more than 30 times. It was a cold-blooded murder. The man who murdered her was under the influence of drugs. He was her sister's boyfriend, and according to the talk, she did not want him to be her sister's boyfriend. And they argued about it and the drug addict pulled out a knife and killed her. And not content with having killed her, he continued stabbing her until she was surrounded by a pool of blood. But the police arrived quickly and handcuffed him and took him and her sister in, so they would testify as to what had happened.

I had never seen a murder. It was very shocking. It was the news of the day. Reporters arrived and many federal, state, and municipal patrol cars and they called SEMEFO [*Servicio Medico Forense*, Forensic Medical Services] so they would take away the corpse. Well, that gave me even greater impetus to leave this *colonia* (Miraflores).

At times I saw gangs fighting against one another. They were from various neighborhoods. I was no longer happy in this house, because it didn't even have a door, and we were at risk that someone would enter to hide.

But, fortunately, nothing happened while we lived there. The only thing that happened is that they stole all the clothing I had washed one afternoon after I arrived from selling newspapers. I had hung it up so it would dry overnight. But what was my surprise when I got up in the morning to take it in and it wasn't there. I was incredulous. I went to the other yards that were near the back entrance. And I saw nothing. I was very angry because they were new clothes that we had bought for the children, and their school uniforms, and even more. It did not seem fair to me that they had robbed me. I still cannot believe it happened. It was all the new clothing that we had bought for them. My poor little children were left without clothes.

That's how it was. I didn't make a scandal. The neighbors did not know what had happened. That's how it was. But not many days went by when a *señora* passed by while I was making dinner and asked me if my clothing had disappeared. And I told her yes, and she said she knew who had stolen it. "It was a woman who likes to go around robbing things. If you like I will tell you where she lives and you go there before she sells it. She is a neighborhood thief. Two days ago I saw her passing by my house with a sack and even asked her where she was going with it. And she answered that she was going to steal some clothing she saw hanging out. And since I saw you hanging out clothing I presumed that she was going to arrive at night."

I didn't want to go to her and protest. But during this time my two eldest sons asked permission to go to play the mechanical games that were nearby the house, and I let them go while I prepared dinner. Then, my eldest son (Toño) arrived and said, "Mama, I now know who robbed the clothes. And she is wearing a blouse of yours and my uniform pants."

"Really, Toño. Don't be telling lies."

"No, mama, she is wearing a blouse that I have seen, no way I am mistaken, and my pants. If you want to, let's go before she goes home."

"Fine, let's go. Let's see if it is true what you are telling me."

And yes, what was my surprise, there was the girl. And when she saw me she became nervous. Since she had seen me in the house she knew who I was. Then I demanded that she return the clothes to me and I threatened to call the police. I arranged for us to go to her house. But she only played the fool in looking for the clothing. And her mother said to me, "*Señora*, she is not going to return it to you because most surely she had sold it by now and she took it to a friend she has. If you like I can give you the address where she is. It's that she is crafty. I am so tired of telling her that she stop thieving. I no longer know what to do with her. She gets together with pure addicts. I have hit her and she leaves the house for a few days and then comes back."

I said to her, "Look, *señora*, whatever you can do. What hurts me is that it was almost all of my children's new clothing and their school uniforms. Even so, let her keep the clothing if she took it to her friend. I don't want it anymore and even less if they put it on and we could get some kind of disease. I don't want it. But, this is for sure, that she does not come close to my house again because if she does I will not be responsible for what happens. If she comes, I will inform the police."

And then I spoke to the girl, "Don't be an idiot (*pendeja*), you know very well where you have it."

And her mother says, "I am very ashamed, *señora*. I no longer know what to do with her."

"Don't worry, *señora*. I am just warning her that she not get close to my house, because we are not alone. She must know the Zapatas. They are my relatives and they know about the problem and they will not hold back from doing something. And I am telling you seriously. It is not a threat. It is a warning." I knew it was not true what I was saying to the *señora* as concerns my relatives doing something, but I had to use someone to protect me.

Well I never saw the girl again. I guess she went to steal in another *colonia*. But it was rarely that she went alone, according to the woman who told me she had stolen the clothing.

That is what happened to me in Colonia Miraflores. Everything else was insignificant. There are times that things happen to one, so one knows how to value what one has. Maybe I had not realized that something was going to happen to me, or we live without realizing it, or we don't want to realize it, and then something happens to wake us up about all that we have.

At that time I lived like a robot and I did everything because it was my routine. I didn't do anything with enthusiasm. I came back tired from selling newspapers and it was my responsibility to make dinner everyday, to get my children's uniforms ready, arrange their beds so they could sleep in them, and next day awake early to make them breakfast and go to sell newspapers. And it was like that every day.

I believed all people were good. Because of this I was confident that nothing could stop me, that all that surrounded me was fine. But we must always distrust even our own shadow—one does not know when it might betray us. It is very painful to know this, but it is true, and there are many other cases like this one.

Afterwards I got experience. I washed clothing early and took it down before we slept. And as the song says, "The burro is not unfriendly, the beatings made her so, made her so." The same thing happened with my older children when they left the house without permission. I had to be mindful of what could happen to them. There are mothers who are not careful of their children. Because of this they turn out badly: because their mothers do not know who their friends are or what they are learning on the street. Of course when they have good examples, no matter who they go around with they remain steadfast in being good. Currently there is so much delinquency and drug addition that in order to get a *peso* to buy drugs, they go as far as to kill someone. They do not know what they are doing. Just to buy drugs.

There was a case in the same Colonia Miraflores on the street down from us in an abandoned house. This is what I found out. I didn't see it but it came out in the newspapers that they had raped a young girl, barely 14 years old. And almost next to the house, if you can call it a house where we lived.

There was a *señora* who sold marijuana—but this was her problem. I went out to the yard and saw her. I greeted her, nothing more.

I have never liked to get involved in problems. This for sure, if they touch my puppies--my children--I am like a lioness in defending them. They good thing is that they also did not like to become involved in fights. When they grew up they did have fights, but this was due to drinking. But it has not happened that the police took them in for fighting. I told them clearly that I would defend them provided that there was some justification, but for going around drunk, don't think that I am going to present my foolish face. (They were sometimes in jail for going around drunk or having alcohol on their breath, especially Gustavo). They know better. And with all the more reason if they were driving. Better that the police take them in than that they cause an accident. I am indeed not in agreement with this. It seems that the police have arrested them for drunk driving, but they are only in jail one or who hours then they let them go. But they have never mentioned it to me. I know from talking to their friends, or simply tell their sisters that they are going to pay the fine. [Their sisters lent them money to pay the fines in these cases]. But they say nothing until I find out. The only think they tell me is that they don't want me to be worried and get ill. But this didn't happen often.

One of many days after I arrived home from vending and was making dinner for my children, the federal police arrived and surrounded the house in Colonia Miraflores, and I was very frightened. And my children began to cry. They thought the police were going to take me away, because they were shouting for me to come out. But they didn't say my name. Because of this I did not go out. But when one of them approached the door, and then another, and the others with guns in hand, it was obvious that I got frightened and most all because I feared they would do something to my children. And then I asked them what was up, and they asked me if Doris was there, and said don't be stupid. They claimed that I had hidden her.

"If you like, come in and check. I don't even know who she is. The only ones here are my children."

Then they came in and didn't find anything because we didn't even have furniture. What we had were the old mattresses my children slept on and a carpet that had been thrown out on which Adolfo and I slept so that the stones [in the dirt floor] didn't hurt us.

And very pained, according to them, they apologized for having arrived in this way, but it was the address they had been given. And it turned out that it was the house beside the one where we lived. That's where this Doris lived. And without my knowing it, she dedicated herself to rob stores like OXXO [a Mexican 7-11] and gasoline stations.

And she lived with her mother, who was named Severina—a well-dressed women whose fingers were always full of rings. And she didn't know what her daughter was doing. This girl, Doris, had two children, a girl and a boy, and they used to play with Guillermo who was the same age. And Doris's mother engaged in bringing marijuana from Sinaloa so you daughter would sell it. Well they were looking for her and I imagine that someone talked to the chief of police and the police went to that house and took away the older woman and so-called "Doris." And the children were left crying. And an aunt of theirs arrived and took them away.

And they--Doris and Severina--were in jail for some years, because when we left they were still imprisoned. Later I found out from my cousin, the one who visited me in the *colonia* where I now live, that they had gotten out of jail and the *señora* had died and her daughter had been killed trying to rob a gas station. And the aunt kept the niece and nephew. But the story was repeated when the girl got older, and the boy as well. The girl grew up and went around robbing people and robbing stores, and the son dedicated himself to selling drugs, and they continue to do so. This *colonia* was very conflict ridden.

What was good is that we got our children out of there, even though Toño liked

going to a store and playing on the game machines. But then it happened that one night

he arrived at 9 p.m. and the police that were guarding the school brought him to me.

And one of them said, "I brought you your son. Don't worry yourself, I am taking care

of him." Or even the very bad boys would bring him and say to me, "Here is your son."

And since they knew my relatives and knew us, we never had any problems with them.

Now I will tell about our selling newspapers, our first job in Mexicali.

Although the first day the press gave us only 100 newspapers to sell, when we returned the following day the man in charge told us he was going to give us 350, because the news was very good and there were no other evening papers. Some men had just robbed a bank and the newspapers were selling like newly baked bread. Well, we left running to the crossroads that we had chosen the day before (Sanchéz Taboada) even though I don't say I was very brave. Not at all, because since the offspring of the rich people of the area were not accustomed to see anyone selling newspapers in their neighborhood, the cars ran us down, and I had to run to the sidewalk to avoid being hit.

And so we began to sell 100 newspapers and up to 3,500 between *La Voz de la Frontera*, and in the afternoon *El Centinela* and *Novedades* together with *La Voz*. And more children began to sell on weekends and my children also went to vend on weekends. Every one had his/her place to sell. They sold near the IMSS clinic that was close to our distribution base. [IMSS, the *Instituto Mexicano de Seguro Social*, is the hospital and clinic complex for formal sector workers]. And the stop sign where I sold near the press of *La Voz* fell to Magali.

At this time there was the Imperial Dairy [*Lechera Imperial*] where Magali vended and since cars and persons came to buy milk they bought the newspaper from her and they gave her tips. And I dedicated myself to deliver the papers to houses: A hundred newspapers every day, carrying them on my head, rolling them up, and throwing them into the garden. And they paid me on weekends. And Adolfo's yield was 200 newspapers, hawking them on the streets and watching over all of the children who vended with us so that nothing would happen to them while they were selling on the street. Because once some people had robbed them of the newspapers, and Adolfo wanted to make sure this did not happen again, so they wouldn't be charged--because Adolfo had to pay the press for all of the missing newspapers. Or people robbed the children of the money. And Adolfo had to watch over our children as well, to see how many newspapers they had yet to sell. And at a certain time, he gathered the children up and took each child to his/her house.

And so the parents were happy and with pleasure they let them go to sell because in order to take along so many children Adolfo had to buy a car. Well now some waited for him at home and others came to play for a while with my children.

And the relatives that ran us off from the house wanted to have the same closeness with us as before, but now it was not the same. Because when we changed to the house I have mentioned, they did not want to provide even a little water to wash the dishes. And now that they saw we were beginning to generate money as well as work for other families, they wanted a way to re-conciliate with us. But now it was not the same. Everything was changing. A neighbor offered us water whenever we needed it and however much we wished. And my children began to want to go to vend. Adolfo changed their schedule in the same school. And they sold the newspapers in the afternoon and went to school in the morning and Adolfo and I went both in the morning and in the evening.

Of the children that helped us—there were about 40—some went to school in the morning and others went in the afternoon and they wanted to go to vend. In this way we shared the newspapers.

There was also a *señor* who lived on the street behind where we lived who brought children to vend newspapers, but they didn't like going with him. They said he was very crooked, that he told them that there was money missing for the sales, that they would have to replace it with their tips or they would remain without pay. They nicknamed him "the pregnant burro" because, they said, he was skinny and big bellied. And when the children accompanied Adolfo, the *señor* got angry. And Adolfo said that if he said anything to them, that they tell him, and that he would say something to shut him up. And the children, playfully, said "The pregnant burro versus Tizoc." That is what they called Adolfo. Tizoc was an Aztec Indian. Because Adolfo began to comb his hair forward and they told him he looked like Tizoc, the one in the movie.

And so this was our routine as newspaper vendors. And I took Guillermo, my youngest son, along and I put him to bed on top of the newspapers. And Gustavo, my second youngest son, as well. And people came by and saw them sleeping and said to me that I give them the children so that they could go to sleep in their homes where it was cooler. [Temperatures can reach 120 degrees in the summer months in Mexicali.] They were people from the same Colonia Nueva of the richest that there were on the Avenida Reforma and Calle I, on the very corner where Magali and I vended.

The head of the state police, Francisco Palao Navarro and his bodyguards lived there. They also took care of us and told us "If you see something or if someone says anything to you, tell us immediately." But fortunately nothing grave happened to us. The people respected us a lot because it seemed very strange to them that we were hawking newspapers.

We had almost 40 kids selling, apart from ourselves. And Adolfo now was an independent distributor and he gave them the newspapers and later charged for them. It was not for a salary, because those at the press trusted us very much. And every Christmas they gave us newspapers for free so we could sell them--to everyone who vended the whole year. And the kids were very content. And the children said, "We

are not going to get anything because the pregnant burro robbed us of part of the sales."
And Adolfo answered that, "No, that all the money from sales is part of your Christmas
and if you want to vend them or to go home, it is each one's choice."

And he encouraged them, "I am not going to take anything away from you, but
bring your mothers a little present, because they deserve it, of for your siblings. You
are not going to spend it all. It has to be shared. And go on and vend. Don't be
annoying."

And when they finished vending he took them to eat tacos or to eat *menudo* at
the municipal market. Well, they were happy with us. It was a way to keep them
content with selling. And they said among themselves, "With Tizoc we are well off."
And when we announced that we were going to leave this house, they became sad. But
Adolfo told them, "But don't think you are going to escape from me. I am going to
come for you at your homes."

And so it was that we were selling newspapers with these children until we
stopped vending. By then they were older and each went their own way to work at
something else. And later we contracted other children. They became close to us just
like those we had before. Some left because their parents didn't want to let them sell
for fear of an accident. And when we changed *colonias* some of the youngsters who
had worked selling newspapers came to visit—by then some were married—and others
we saw by chance when we were passing through and we greeted one another. Those
who visited us remembered what Tizoc—as they called Adolfo—was like. That he took
care of them and how they made him angry at times, but most of all how he took them
to eat or he brought them tacos and sodas. One of the young men continues visiting us
to this day. He became a good friend of my son Marcelo, my third eldest son, since
they were together in the barracks when they became recruits.

This was a stage of our daily life in Colonia Miraflores of Mexicali. And I have to say of our relatives, I never returned to visit them. But my offspring did return, because I never inculcated resentment against them. Except one of the cousins behaved very well. Upon seeing that I didn't have any money, when he went to work in the fields of Calexico upon returning he would buy a gallon of milk and would give it to me so that I could give it to my children. And he took them to buy tortillas and eggs so I could give it to them. I am very thankful to him also for what he did for us. He comes to the house now and then and brings us sweets—caramels—that he makes and I take care of him as he deserves. He is the youngest of my aunt's—my mother's sister's—family.

And I thank them for the time they gave us shelter, but not for the way they acted with me. Principally because being direct relations they did not behave well with me—because they did not want to provide me with water, not even to wash dishes.

Now thanks to the invasions of residential lots the then governor Xicantencatl Levya Mortera permitted, we have a house and now the lots are legalized. We have all the necessary services, such as electricity, running water, and sewerage, and it did not cost much to obtain these services. Our *colonia* is lacking in paved roads, but we do have two streets that are paved, the street where the kindergarten is and the street passing the primary school. But this is another story.

We stayed in Miraflores 3 years, and then there was the invasion [about which more will be related in the next three chapters]

Because some of the children the children who went and asked us to sell newspapers went to school in the morning and others in the afternoon, we had to assign them the time they could go to vend. By then we had the concession for the Tijuana weekly newspaper *El Zeta*. In the beginning the other person who sold it before us was selling only 35 copies. And we came to sell 1,500 every week, because the clients were asking us for more and more. Now all the hawkers that we brought sold it, and since they earned a little more they were very enthused. And also the buyers left them tips. They were very happy at this time.

Even the municipal president came and bought what he called the newspaper of newspapers from us. All of the newspapers we sold they bought from Magali and they gave her a good tip, probably because it seemed curious to them to see a little girl shouting out when no one else was. The other hawkers only displayed the newspapers. But we called out so that people would turn our way and be motivated to buy them. Even the Bishop came and bought a newspaper and later he told us that we should deliver it to his house and he would pay for it each month. We had to finance it for a month, but when he paid us, he gave us a good tip.

Well, it went well with us because we as a family kept 30 percent of the earnings as well as the tips they gave us. Women came and gave Magali little presents. She got the most tips. It was in Colonia Nueva where almost all the offspring of the settlers of Mexicali lived. And the chief of police came out and bought the newspaper and left her the change. *La Voz* cost 3 pesos and he left her the change from 100. There was also another girl who passed by once or twice a week and bought the newspaper and left Magali 100 pesos—and told her that she should keep the change for herself, it was fine.

And it fell to Aida to sell at the IMSS and the nurses took her in to breakfast in the kitchen. And one doctor (female) liked her very much and she supplied her with vitamins and told her, "Take them so you will become even prettier than you are."

A worker in a clinic—I don't remember its name—also bought clothing for Toño and she took him to try out shoes in a shoe store and bought them for him. People also arrived all the time with bags of baked goods and toys that they gave to Indira, who was nicknamed, *la gorda*. And people gave things to almost all of my offspring. The manager of the Imperial Dairy gave us a gallon of milk daily, and ice cream for all the vendors. Because of this all the children followed us around and asked us for work because they said we had good luck. Of course we also asked them that they try to sell all the newspapers that we supplied them with and thus not have to return them.

We also brought along girls who wanted to earn money to take to school. But we stationed them at stop signs so that nothing would happen to them. And we counseled them the same as our daughters, that "If someone calls you over from a car that is not close by you don't go. That they get out of the car if they want to buy the newspaper. You don't go to anyone else except those that pass by the stop sign in their cars. Or you can bring the newspaper to a *señora* that cannot cross the street, but that they are aged women whom you have seen before. Understand?"

"Yes, we understand. It's fine."

"Now let's go so that you know where you will be vending. And when you are finished with vending come to this crossroads where my daughter Magali is. Here is the distribution base and here you will all have to be so we can go home."

There were times that a child would not arrive and we would all have to go to look for him. At times they went to spend their tips in a store with game machines that swallow up money ("*maquinas tragamonedas*"). And there they were playing. Well then we knew where they were and we stopped this custom of spending their tips. And what Adolfo did was to count the money from sales, and he gathered up their tips, and when we arrived at their houses, he gave each one a little bag with the money. And later they themselves handed their tips over and they said to Adolfo, "It is stupid that I earned my tips and spent them and at home I have all my tips saved up and what I earn from sales I give to my mother so that she will buy us food and clothing at the *tianguis*. There is a lot of good clothing, Adolfo, almost new."

"Now you see, my stubborn ones, that which I am doing is not bad." Because Adolfo gave each one 25 percent of the sales, and he took 5 percent from each child. He did not give the same amount to all of them, but according to how many they could sell.

There were youngsters who could sell 150 newspapers between 6 and 9:30 or 10 in the morning. When it didn't go so well, they finished at 11, but they sold almost everything. In the event that some newspaper remained—they were 3 or 5—it was because the youngsters had to go to prepare to attend school. And the second shift began with us. Some left and others we brought in in the afternoon.

We sold fewer newspapers in the afternoon, because the number of newspapers was less, and so they handed over only a few, maybe 450. But what also made us strong was the weekly *Zeta*. We could sell this periodical all during the week. And besides we sold magazines like *TV Novela* and fashion magazines. But these Adolfo and I vended in offices of whatever type, such as banks, furniture stores, all the offices in the government center. The people asked us to put them aside—we just went and delivered them.

Then the next day we had the same routine. Arrive at 5 in the morning and be the first to sell. Because children were waiting for us at the press's office—those who came by bus--because not all lived in the same Colonia Miraflores. Others lived in the following colonias: Benito Juárez, Roma, Constitución, and Republica Mexicana.

They were the children that we gave the first newspapers to, for having arrived earlier. We brought children, and others not so much children, between 9 and 16, and even so the older ones were more difficult to contract because they didn't want us to give them advice. And they said, "Now we know what we have to do. Go and sell the '*papiro*'(that is what they called the newspaper) and report to the *señora* that notes down how many are left, and when you come you collect the money," they said to Adolfo.

"O.K., get going. And be very careful that you don't come out with that you couldn't sell today, so that you could go to the little game machines. I am going to be watching you."

"Until then, *papí*. Not until 11, and you are going to collect the money at the house, because we are going to bathe to go to school and we don't have time to wait for you."

"That's fine. Just let me know if you have newspapers left over, and how many, so I can charge you later. And don't come up with that you have lost the money. If I forgive nothing with my children, why forgive you? Once or twice I have forgiven you but now you have become accustomed, and don't be arguing with me. Go on and vend and whoever doesn't want to come, just tell me, so I don't go to your house and waste my time. When all is said and done, there are more kids who want to vend. You chose if you want me to give you the job. We'll see each other later, because I have to go to deliver my newspapers, because even if you don't believe it, I also sell and deliver. And I have to be supervising who is at their crossroads. And also some smart aleck shows up and robs you of money or of the '*papiro*' as you call it."

"Tizoc, when will you take us to eat tacos or to the city park to see the animals there?"

"Well, ask your parents' permission and this Sunday I will take you. But you have to sell all the newspapers I am giving you. If not, there will be no outing. Are we clear on this?"

"Whatever you say, boss. Now we are going to behave well."

And when the weekend arrived he took them to amuse themselves a little and took our children as well. How much they needed him also! He had to make two trips in the van to take all of them, because not all would fit. And so he kept them happy.

It was a matter of two or three hours of having fun. Then he took them home. Their parents trusted us because we took good care of them. But it looked like an army with so many kids, and my children who went along with them—and even more so when they gathered together at the newspaper distribution point. People passed by and stared. And because Adolfo had a loud voice, the people thought he was scolding the kids--but he was only giving them instructions.

And when we moved from Colonia Miraflores , some of the children had to come to us by bus, and they arrived a little late. So we lowered the quantity of newspapers they had to sell, so that they could sell all of them, or almost all. Of 1,500 daily there remained only 30 or 40 and at times less.

That was our daily routine. This in the morning and then another group came in the afternoon. But then there was less work and we didn't have to struggle with so many children, because there were less of them. We gave them few newspapers. We took only 350 newspapers, *El Centinela*, and furthermore it was thinner and they finished selling them early. They worked from 1 to 3 in the afternoon, and then they were free. And we took the children who sold in the afternoon on an outing on Sunday, because the newspaper did not come out that day.

There were men who also asked us for work, and we gave it to them. But they were a bit lazier than the children and lasted only a few days before they left. They despaired because people did not buy the newspaper quickly and did not return. But that was what this work was like. At times the sales went fast and at times not so fast. We had to have patience, but what could be sold, was sold. It was a matter of waiting and shouting out and resting some five or ten minutes, and continuing on.

There were *señores* who passed by and bought as many as five newspapers together. Why we did not know, but it didn't matter to us. The goal was to sell them. Maybe so we could finish fast, or maybe to give to their friends. We never knew.

One *señora,* very elegant, used to walk by where Magali vended and buy a newspaper--but then give it back to us. She didn't even leaf through it. And she even left us the change. That happened daily. Most probably this was a way of giving Magali money in a way that she would accept it. We called the *señora* the Duchess, because she arranged her hair like they did long ago. She had very long hair but always well groomed and pulled back with very pretty hair combs. And she was a *señora* aged 65 or 70. We had never seen a woman like her. She lived on the street in front of *La Voz de la Frontera.* Her house was not very pretty, but it had a well-kept garden.

And also there was a woman who earned her living by washing and ironing other people's clothing and who lived near where we vended. She always brought us cold water to drink. She said it was so we would hydrate ourselves when it was very hot.

Other people brought gifts for Memo. They brought him ice cream. He was still only a little boy and spent much time sleeping on top of the newspapers. And later he wanted to vend, so I gave him two or three newspapers so that he had them in his hands as though he were vending. And people bought them. He was very content, and he said, "*Mamí*, now I know how to vend and they gave me a tip. Should I give it to you?"

"No, my son, it is for you. But the money that they gave you for the sale, yes, you should give it to me. Because it is to pay for them [the newspapers] and so that they will give us others so that we can keep going, O.K.?"

"Yes, *mamí*, but I want more because they run out quickly."

"Well here you are seated on top of them [the pile of newspapers]. You can take those that people ask you for, but be careful that they don't go away without paying. And if you don't know how to make change, call me, so that I give it to them. And also, if they say anything insulting, tell me. Keep sitting on top of the newspapers in case it gets windy, so they don't blow away."

Well Gustavo, a little older, now wanted to go to sell at the IMSS, which was located about 3 blocks from where we kept the newspapers. He now knew how to make change and it was safer because the doctors gave him permission to vend them inside and stop by all the consultation rooms—just like Aida. There they worked and took care of each other until Adolfo arrived and brought them to me. Then he went for the others so that I could take them home and get them ready for school. Toño and Carlos were by then in secondary school [junior high school]. There was no problem with them because the school was just down the street (in Miraflores). The others went about three blocks away—the school was in Colonia Roma. We lived only one block away from that *colonia.*

When Antonio went to sell on the street running past the border between Calexico and Mexicali—some call it the international street, but its name is Avenida Colón, he passed the time watching those who crossed the border illegally though a hole in the fence that divided the two countries. It was a cyclone fence. They took care that there were no "Border Patrol" vans or police from Mexicali. At first he found it amusing how they crossed, and later he himself advised them that neither of the patrols [U.S. Border Patrol or Mexican immigration officials] were present and he told them, "Now, cross quickly. No one is coming."

He told us that during the time he was selling newspapers, between 15 and 20 people crossed, including both women and men. At times they were accompanied by children, and they ran across. And he didn't know if they captured them later, but he saw that they hid themselves in houses close to the borderline. And that happened daily, and he helped them to cross.

It was easier before. Later they discovered that the fence was torn and the authorities went to block it. Even so, people jumped over it and crossed. There were people that got stuck and others pulled them across so they wouldn't be discovered. Toño told us that he felt sorry about how they were all dirty since they had just arrived by train from the south, and how a *señor* that always passed by gave him oranges so that those who were crossing would have something in their stomachs. [The *señor* gave Toño oranges, so that Toño would pass them on to those who were crossing.] He told me, "This is why I help them to cross and let's hope the *migra* does not capture them. I feel badly for the children they have with them. And I don't know if someone is waiting for them on the other side to take them to some relative. But, *mamí*, what need to they have to risk going with their children when they could pass alone themselves, and later send for their family? And then imagine how much the coyotes [people smugglers] are going to charge them if they don't just rob them and abandon them and take away from them the only money that they have and without being able to reach their destination. May God grant that they have luck and that nothing happens to them."

I asked Toño, "Aren't you afraid that the police will do something to you if they see you helping people to cross?"

And he replied, "No, because I always pay attention to see that they are not coming. It has happened that they asked me if I have seen what is happening at the hole and I answer that I don't even pay attention because I am working. And then they leave. They don't do anything to me because I am not crossing them [those crossing the border]. I am just helping them to cross. And the police know me and even buy the newspaper from me."

Antonio (Toño) is the eldest of my offspring. Back then he was 16 years old. He was in the last year of secondary school when we arrived in Mexicali. And there was no place in school for him or for Marcelo, one of my three youngest children. And Toño couldn't attend until the following school year. They were my right hand when we ran out of money. When we lived in my relatives' house we went out to collect tin cans. At that time beer cans were made of tin, not of aluminum as they are now. And we filled a wheelbarrow that the man we sold them to lent us. And so I bought a few groceries, a bag of pasta and tortillas. And so they had a little to eat.

Once we began to sell newspapers we were better off economically and we began to eat better. But then we changed houses, that they practically lent us, because we only had to pay 150 *pesos* a month in rent. By now we had enough to buy the children the items they needed for school. It is sad to remember things, but also nice, because it taught us to value what we have and what we do. If we had not had the work with the newspapers and with my children participating, we would never have appreciated anything. And with this work they had enough to eat and to study the little that they know.

Magali selling newspapers

My two eldest daughters, after finishing secondary school, went to study in a rural teachers training school in the state of Chihuahua. There were approximately 50 students from various states, but my daughters were the only ones from Baja California. And at that time my daughter Magali was 15 years old and my daughter Indira was 16 years old. They decided to go. They said they wanted to avoid being around their father for a while, because he didn't let them go anywhere. That he was very strict with them.

But Magali told me that if she returned one day and there was no money in the house, she would go and sell newspapers again, because she never was ashamed of that work. That it was as dignified as any other. When she started selling newspapers she was 10 years old and she said that in the beginning she was nervous about it, but later on she wasn't—she said that it seemed natural to her.

And Indira was more daring. She didn't care if anyone made fun of her. She knew we were poor and that no one was going to feed us, not the neighbors or anyone else. And so she began vending. As soon as they gave her her first pile of newspapers, she asked, "Where am I going to go to vend?"

Aida was shyer. She almost didn't speak. And I told her, "Your papa is going to place you in the social security hospital [IMSS], and don't move away from there. If you finish vending stay there until he stops by for you."

Aida was always the quietist of my three daughters and still is, even though she is now married. But she also was forceful about selling newspapers. She sold between 100 and 150 newspapers daily and received very good tips from the doctors, the nurses, and the people who went to the hospital for a consultation. And as I mentioned previously, they enthusiastically prescribed her vitamins, and if they saw she had a little cold, they prescribed medications so that she would get better. When Aida began vending she was 9 years old.

At times when we were waiting for Adolfo in the hospital's garden my children amused themselves climbing the trees that were there, while their father finished selling the newspapers that were left over from Aida's share. And one day it occurred to my quietist daughter—Aida—to climb up a tree, while shouting "I am a monkey." And she fell down into the grass that was full of manure, and she was covered with it. Well we had to bathe her right there.

The good thing was that we always brought along powdered soap to wash our hands after vending because the money we handled made our hands dirty. And we had to throw the clothing that Aida was wearing in the garbage. And Adolfo loaned her the shirt he was wearing. And all of my children were laughing and laughing, and Aida crying. Besides the hurt from falling, she was embarrassed about having been covered by manure. And from then on when we referred to her we called her "the little monkey." And she answered as though we had called her by her name. At times they called her "monkey" and at times "little monkey"—but she became accustomed to this nickname.

My cousin, he who visits us, nicknamed her "the cricket" because when we arrived she was very thin and he said she looked like a cricket. But she now knows he said it with affection. We did not allow other children to call her nicknames, because they were going to do it to make fun of her, and I did not allow other children to ridicule her. My children avoided doing such things, as I taught them from the beginning.

Now thanks to the invasions of residential lots the then governor Xicantencatl Levya Mortera permitted, we have a house and now the lots are legalized. We have all the necessary services, such as electricity, running water, and sewerage, and it did not cost much to obtain these services. Our *colonia* is lacking in paved roads, but we do have two streets that are paved, the street where the kindergarten is and the street passing the primary school. But this is another story.

The house where we now live was a lot we acquired through the invasion. We learned about it through a *señor* who worked as a gardener nearby where we worked selling newspapers. And he asked if we rented or had our own house. And we answered him that we were living in a borrowed house. Then he mentioned that on the highway to San Felipe there was an invasion of lots. That if we wanted to go, there still were lots available and that we should go so that they gave us one. And if there were none remaining, he had acquired three lots, and that he would pass one of them on to us. But that we should go before someone else invaded them. And so it was that we went that day after vending the newspapers.

But since the *señor* was not there this day, we didn't know who could give us information about how one could acquire a lot. Because no one--since they were very busy measuring their lots and putting up ropes--paid any attention to us. And we left and I commented to Adolfo that most probably there were none. But then he told me, "For some reason the *señor* told us we should come, then there still are. And, remember, that he told us if there were none he could pass on one of those that he had put aside. The bad thing is that we did not see him today, but tomorrow when we see him, we will tell them that no one wanted to tell us if there were lots available or not.

And if the *señor* tells us that he will pass one on to us, we will go and clean it immediately. And we will begin to defend it, if only with cardboard and some stilts, and we will go daily so they get used to seeing us, and will trust us."

"Well, it seems good to me. It will be useful if we take along the kids when they get out of school so that they help us to throw away the garbage that we collect." And so we went. We saw the *señor* and he told us that he would pass one of his lots on to us.

The next day we went with this plan in mind to sell newspapers and we saw the *señor* and he asked us if we had gone. And yes, that there were still lots. We mentioned to him that no one wanted to inform us of anything. And he said, "Well tomorrow we will see each other there and I will give you one of my lots that my son separated out. Not even crazy does he want to take part in the invasion—he doesn't want problems if the police throw us out of there."

Thus we decided. The next day we went again and we met with the *señor* and he said he was going to give us one of the lots. Then he told us which it was. And when we were cleaning up and putting up the take to leave it marked off, he who supposedly had been named leader—because nobody felt they were capable of speaking—arrived. I began by speaking nicely to this *señor,* Santiago Goméz García, nicknamed Gori. It was he who was in charge of giving lots to anyone he wished. And when he saw us he asked us, "Who put you into this lot?"

And Adolfo answers "*Señor* Ángel."

And he answered, "I don't even know that *señor*. Because this lot has been kept aside for other people and there are no more lots. All the rest have been assigned. So I am sorry."

And *don* Ángel answered him, "If they are here it is because they are poor. They are living in a little borrowed house and I invited them to come. Because of this I am passing on this lot, because I selected it for one of my sons. Since he didn't want it I am passing it on to them."

And Adolfo told him, "No, *señor* Ángel. Don't involve yourself in problems with this *señor*. He is going to tell us where there is one."

And Santiago stared at him and he said, "Well there is one that no one has wanted. If you want it, go and clean it up."

"Just tell me where it is and I'll take charge."

And he pointed it out, "Look at that lot." Well that was a lot that nobody wanted because it was filled with garbage and bones of dead animals. It also had a kind of fiber that if you handled it, it fell apart and stung. It was like fiberglass.

Well, so we went to clean the lot. We thanked *don* Ángel, son-in-law of a couple who went to live on his lot. And we were cleaning the lot daily. And we contracted a bulldozer to finish cleaning and to level off the land. Also there were stretches of salt or saltpeter. No one knew what it was.

We began to take thick poles and we made a little tent where we stayed. And we installed ourselves there. At least at this time our youngest children had still not entered school. And the others we had in school.

At this time there was a lot of wind. And I took cans of sardines to eat with salted crackers and what we ate was pure dirt, because one couldn't eat anything. I remember that my little boy, covered with dust, said, *"Mamí,* I can't see. Dirt has entered my eyes and my body is itching." And his body was filled with welts.

I guess it was from the fiber that had entered the ground that the bulldozer had dislodged. I had to bathe him immediately in the canal that surrounded the invasion

80

even before the *colonia* was formed. [These were irrigation canals from which the surrounding fields were watered]. We had a little tent made of old curtains that we found thrown away in the garbage. [There was a garbage dump lining the northern side of the *colonia*]. Now I regretted having gone because there was no end to cleaning. But what we were doing was that we also contracted dump trucks with earth to infill the land, because, as I mentioned, it was the dirtiest.

But because of the need to have somewhere to live, we had to endure. Besides my children were growing up in an environment that was not healthy for them. There was much addiction to drugs in Miraflores and they were indeed happy to get away from those surroundings. And even their teachers counseled them that they tell us to get them out of there, because they were very wholesome children. And Memo [her youngest son] also began to like the place, because he said to me, "*Mamí*, when are we going to the Indian house that you made for me in that place?" He was 5 years old then. Perhaps he believed we were going camping, or he, in his innocence, did not think about it.

And I asked him, "When we build a good house, would you like to live there?"

"Yes, *mamí*, because there is a lot of water and I can go to swim every day. Because here in the house you bathe us very seldom and with just a little water that the neighbors give you. And when we are there my siblings can bathe before they go to sell the newspapers."

"Well I promise you that when they are on vacation from school we will go, because there you will have many friends."

Well when we left Colonia Miraflores, my children became nostalgic because they were going to suffer even more, and above all, they were going to begin a new life.

But they would have to become accustomed, because we were farther away from the work and they would have to go to school further away. We had no schools because we were just beginning to want to form a *colonia*, and all of us in the community were just possessors of lots that did not belong to us.

But so we continued going to sell the newspapers, and the children began to be content. Now they felt they had their own house, even though it was of cardboard and tarpaulins. We began to construct three little rooms that served us as bedrooms and a kitchen while we held the neighborhood meetings to plan what we were going to do so that the government would come and legalize us. But much was lacking.

We had to give Santiago, the self-appointed leader, a quota that he asked of us each week. He said it was for his expenses. It was a piggy bank without a bottom because we could not see when he was going to arrange things through deputy Armando Ruíz Valdéz, medical zoologist, from the PRI. The deputy gave us an orientation when we went to see him in his office.

He told us, "Go right now to the *colonia* and prepare signs and go out to the highway. The governor is going to pass by on his way to San Felipe. Stop him and ask him that he send someone or that he go to the *colonia*."

Because of this we had to name the *colonia*, even though there were very few houses, and those made of cardboard and plastic sheets. And soon we arrived with the same ones who were bringing these things from the Imperial Dairy.

We spread the people out. We were still not very many, but the few that we were went and stood in the middle of the highway. Gori (Santiago) accompanied us and when the beginnings of the governor's train of people appeared there was the deputy. He signaled to us that the governor was following behind. But when governor Xico—

that's what people called him—saw us, he stopped. There was no need to stop him. And he greeted us very kindly and the people greeted him.

And he asked us what motive we had for being there. And we mentioned what we wanted to him and he answered, "Look, right now I am going to a conference I have in San Felipe, but I promise you that tomorrow I will be here in your colonia so that you can tell me about your needs. And take into account that I will give you everything in writing." Then he assured us that he would come to visit us and find a solution to our problems.

"We do not want promises, we want a solution, *señor* governor," one *señora* told him. "We are lacking in everything."

"*Señores*, I am not acquainted with the colonia. What do you say it is called?"

"It is called Unión Lázaro Cárdenas. That is what we called in, in honor of President Lázaro Cardenás del Río [1934-1940], and that is what we want our school that will be constructed here, to be called.

"Well, here I will be tomorrow, I assure you."

And then he left to attend to his obligation and he said to the *señores*, "I will be here."

Well, we left very content, others incredulous, saying that he had said this so we would let him go. "You are going to see that he will not show up, but because of doubts, we have to be on the land where the school will be."

[Because there was another *colonia* in Mexicali called Unión Lázaro Cárdenas, this *colonia* was ultimately named Unión de Residentes Lázaro Cárdenas.]

Well, we silenced those who didn't believe he would come. He brought officials from the State Real Estate Office [*Inmobiliaria del Estado*], representatives from C.C.I.

[*Central Campesina Independiente*, Independent Peasants' Central], his private secretary, and his bodyguards. We now had readied the space where he was going to be. We brought some planks that served as benches and some old tables that we had, and of course the petition that we had ready. And he showed up. He asked us what needs we had, and out of respect we told Gori that he speak for us, since he had named himself as our representative. And we gave the governor the papers that we had brought, that we all had elaborated. The first thing that we asked for was that he regularize our lots—since it was an invasion and we still didn't know what was going to happen if the owner presented a lawsuit.

And he answered us, "Look, that is not going to happen, because I am going to help you, but this is going to some time. And don't be afraid. For this I am here. No one is going to bother you. I want you to know that it was because of this that I brought my secretary, so that he will take note of what we discuss at this meeting. And if there is someone who represents all of you, s/he should show up at my office so I can present a response to your petitions. But first I have to know what situation the land is in."

Gori wanted us to contract for the lots without knowing if the owners were going to look for another piece of land [for the invaders] that was now legalized, and this would take awhile. The *señor* governor spoke very nicely to us and then he said goodbye. But a representative of the C.C.I. stayed behind to tell us that we should affiliate with the alliance that he represented, and that this organization would help us as concerns the petitions we made.

We were in agreement—what we wanted was someone to help us. But upon seeing that Gori didn't do anything except ask us for money—to put gasoline in his car and to buy food—because, he said, he was not working because he was riding around taking care of colonia matters and he did not have enough money to even eat a taco. And we were happy to give the money to him. But we saw no advancements.

We began to protest that it was not fair that he was doing nothing but taking our money. And to make matters even worse, he asked us for money to buy a new motor for his van—because the old one had stopped working since he had to go back and forth to San Luís [San Luís Río Colorado, about 50 miles away in the state of Sonora]. But everything that had to be arranged was here in Mexicali.

And we began to yell, "We are not going to give you anymore money, Gori, because you are simply exploiting us. And how much we believed in you." They asked Adolfo to become the representative. He could shout—it seemed like he had a megaphone!

But there were those who preferred Gori—all of his family and their acquaintances. He was their favorite, but the majority had more power. We did not dismiss him until we saw what he might do. He kept a goldfish in his hand [his cards to his chest] and said he had arranged everything. And we began to say to him that he show us in writing everything that he had arranged, and the responses they gave him. And he told us that this was private, that he would not show us anything, but that everything was advancing, and that the electrical company was going to erect posts for the electricity. This when we didn't have a notion if the government officials had localized the owner of the land that we had invaded.

Then it occurred to us to invite the C.C.I. representative so that he would help us to locate the owner, and he did so. They were two brothers. Their surname was Lerma, and those from the C.C.I. sent an official notice to the governor saying that they had found the owners, and also a notice to the State Real Estate Office so that they would negotiate with them. That way we could contract the lots.

And so we began the struggle. Almost like during the Revolution, we affiliated ourselves to the State Agrarian League (LEA, Liga Agraria Estatal), now C.C.I., but with the same leaders. They just changed the rules so they could dedicate themselves to helping the *colonias populares* or in communities that had problems, such as ours, as well. They helped us a lot during their time, inviting representatives of the official branches that were involved in contracting lots. We were just possessors--not owners.

But in May of 1985, after one year and four months, we invited people from the State Real Estate Office and from C.C.I. to come to the *colonia*. Their representative was Cefernio Saavedra Godínez. And they let us know how things were advancing with the brothers Lerma. And they said that first of all we must form a neighborhood committee [*Comité de Vecinos*]. And they asked us if we had a representative. And Adolfo raised his hand and said it was Santiago (Gori). But the people protested that they didn't want him to be the leader anymore, that he was telling us complete lies, and that he was taking money away from us and didn't even inform us about anything. They wanted someone else.

Well right then the neighborhood committee was formed and by the majority of votes they wanted Adolfo to be president of the *colonia*. But Adolfo had a strategy and he refused to represent the *colonia*. And that was when he told them, "I propose my wife, because she had brought a group of women to arrange for electricity and also taken people to the civic center so that they will bring us water in a water truck. That's why we have water. And as far as electricity is concerned, it is logical that the C.F.E. [*Comisión Federal de Electricidad*, Federal Electricity Commission] is not going to install electricity because there is no paperwork that confirms that the lots are ours. But here are the documents showing what this group has asked for, and the responses."

He showed them to the representatives of the official branches, and the people shouted, "These deserve to be leaders. Let the *señora* be our representative."

I didn't want to because I have never been involved in such projects. It was just that a group of women had followed along with me.

We were a group of approximately 25 women. We were advised by the delegate Armando Ruíz to go to see the regional representative of the C.F.E. so that our petitions could be speeded up and that we tell him of the urgent needs we had. He told us where, and so we went. He--the regional representative--met us with much consideration, but his response was that he could send someone to put in some electric cables, but not for the entire *colonia*. And our response was, "For all the *colonia* or nothing"--because we all needed electricity. And we rejected his response and we had all this down in writing. And when the other people found out what we were doing, they supported us even more. "Then may she be our president." At this time they dismissed Gori and elected me.

And since they wanted a neighborhood committee that was well organized, they elected Adolfo as secretary and some women who were mixed up in the group. And so the neighborhood committee was formed. We took official minutes and everyone endorsed our nominations. And so to work.

From then on the whole committee had to meet to come to agreements and to develop petitions to all the official branches—State Real Estate Office, state government, the Mexicali Commission of Public Services, water, the C.F.E.—where we all knew we had to go. We had to support the C.C.I. because they typed up the petitions for us. We brought them the papers written by hand and they put them on the letterhead of their organization. They said that way they would pay more attention to us. And so we dedicated ourselves to meet every weekend to let the people know how we were getting ahead. And we read them the petitions that we presented to each official branch, and when they were going to give us a response.

At that time the director of the State Real Estate Office was an engineer called Arturo Hernández, and it was he who had received instructions from the governor to give priority to the *colonia*, that they go to measure the lots, and that he call and make an appointment with the owners in order to pay them for their land. And the director said he was going to make them an appointment with the governor, so that they settled with him, since the instructions were from him. Well it went badly for them [the owners, the Lerma brothers], because it seems the governor told them that if they didn't want to sell, now there were people living on those lands, and he wasn't going to transfer them to other *colonias*--if they didn't want to sell, the land would be seized. And that is what happened to these hectares. They had been unused for 40 years. It seems that the owners were very annoyed when they left the governor.

And that was when the engineers from the State Real Estate Office began to ratify the measurements. Only we saved them this work. Everything was good. Only the lots on the border had to be measured, and the engineers measured the meters and gave them to the occupants. Then they drew maps including those lots along the border of the *colonia*. They were some land that a *señora* had bought and these lands had permits to be used as brickyards. And the engineers included these lots in the map of the *colonia* so that those who occupied them could contract for them. I helped the engineers to get the names of each family and add them to the list of possessors.

And I asked the social worker for the State Real Estate Office if they had paid the owners--the Lerma brothers--and she answered me that the State Real Estate Office had confiscated the lands. They had paid them with a check for nine thousand pesos, but the owners had never come to pick it up. Until now nothing is known of them.

The office began to contract the lots on the 10th of July 1985. That day they told me that the licenses for contracts were ready and that I should bring a group of 10 everyday, because they were not going to be able to give contracts to everyone the same day. So that's what we did.

It was two months after having formed the neighborhood committee that we began to contract for the lots. When I was composing the list, along with the social worker, she explained to me clearly, "Ernestina, these lots are going to be contracted by the housewives, whether they are married or not, even if they are single mothers, so that they have a place to live if their husbands abandon them or want to take away the house or whatever they build. That he has no right to do so. These are the boss's instructions and you have to do the same thing. The only exception is if there is some man who lives alone. You have to verify that he has no wife and that his children are grown up. And ask everyone for every proof they have, their identification cards—like IFE, (the federal voting card), which is the principal credential—and birth certificate, in order to compare it with their identification card."

Well I was in a jam over this. Some *señores* had neither an identification card nor a birth certificate. But I left these until the last moment until I could get them some document that would be of value to them. I had to take them to the civil registry so that they would give them a card with their photograph as an official document, and thus could contract for their lots. They were very grateful to me for having helped them, even though after having secured him a contract, one of them sold his house and went somewhere, I don't know where, but he abandoned the *colonia*. It seems he didn't even sell it. He disappeared and a *señora* took over the lot and they did not remove her. And up to the moment she has not been able to put it in her name because it is contracted to the old possessor. She continues paying for water, electricity, and property taxes, but in the name of the *señor*.

Well after I had been president for 2 months, there was a contracting of lots-- they sent me the official documents. I asked Santiago if he would please give me the *colonia*'s seal and the notebook where he listed the money we gave him. As concerns the documents we asked him for that said they were going to put in electricity—they never existed. And he did give me both the seal and the notebook, and I have kept them until today.

After contracting for the lots, we continued to make petitions so that they would install electricity, for which we had to hold a peaceful demonstration, without shouting. We walked slowly to the office where the governor was. His secretary received us very kindly, and the people were very orderly. And we planned not to leave until we got a positive response. There were 200 lots apart from the lots for the kindergarten and for the primary school, thus 200 families. Luckily he always had a good reply for us.

The governor passed by and he asked me what it was we wanted. Now we were talking to him. We showed him our petition. He signed it and said that he would quickly give orders to start. And so it was. We left very content, but some people who were with us commented that he had said this just to get us out of his office. And those who had remained in the *colonia* asked us how it had gone. And the *señoras* answered, "You should have come along to find out. The reply he gave us is that we could not move forward until they began to put up the posts or begin to bring them."

I remember that the audience with the governor was on a Wednesday, and by Thursday the posts began to arrive and we were surprised. "How is it possible that yesterday we were with the governor and now we are going to have electricity! We can't believe it!"

We thought he was playing a joke on us, or that probably it was a mistake—that they had come to the wrong *colonia*. And we had to go to ask the *señores* who drove the trucks with the materials if they had made a mistake. Well they asked us, "Is this the Colonia Unión de Residentes Lázaro Cárdenas?"

"Yes, sir."

"Well we are going to dig pits to fit the poles into and lay the cable work."

And in two months we had electricity in our *colonia*. I don't remember what year it was. It seems to me that it was after two years, in 1987. But now at least we could buy a fan to blow away the mosquitos. There were masses of them. We were near a canal that carried water to irrigate the fields that surrounded the colonia on two sides.

But what was strange is that we had streetlights before we became owners of our lots. When they switched on the streetlights the first time, I didn't even know they were lit when I heard an uproar in the street in front of my house. And I said to Adolfo, "There are a lot of people shouting at me and mentioning my name. What do they want? Hopefully it is not bad news."

When I went out to see what was happening they began to should, "Hurrah Ernestina! Ernestina, Ernestina, ra, ra, ra."

"And this? Why so much fuss?"

"Haven't you noticed that we now have lights switched on in the street?"

And then I looked and jumped with joy and I told them, "See, our efforts have been worthwhile. And there is still much to fight for, to have everything we need."

By then the State Real Estate Office was aiding us by sending water trucks. Later the same governor gave us a water truck that we would be in charge of. And he told me clearly, "I am going to provide it, but you are going to give it maintenance though leveling a quota, or however you can." Then he told me to go for it in a state warehouse and immediately they put my name on the [temporary] papers.

I was asking that they support us by supplying us with water through the municipality or by one of the firemen's water trucks. But I didn't figure that they were going to lend us a water truck exclusively for the *colonia*. And I went to get it at the state warehouse. And so we began to work, taking water to each family for a donation of 2 pesos for each 200 liter barrel, in order to pay for its maintenance. And despite as much as it was cared for it ground us down (broke our teeth) and we had to take it to the mechanic's shop and get it back quickly because people could not go without water.

Or at times we lost water because of holes in the tank. All of these things we had to repair. At times the money we collected was insufficient. We had to pay with the money we earned from newspaper sales, because even if we asked for a donation, some families had still not come to live in the *colonia*, and there was not enough money. And also there were families who did not have enough money to fill their barrels. Our obligation was to leave them water, and this water was then free to them. We did not ask anything from elderly people. The neighborhood committee had agreed we should do this—supply them with water for free.

Then also, no one wanted the responsibility of driving the water truck because as we told them, we could not pay them a salary, because we could not collect that much money. And we had the expenses for maintain the truck. And at times people did not have the money to contribute. My son Carlos is the one who took on the responsibility for driving the water truck, with the reservation that he would drive it for about 3 hours during the week until the time came for him to go to school--he was in high school--but that on Saturdays and Sundays he would have more time.

We also had the expenses for gasoline. In sum, in one way or another it involved expenditures. But we had to verify the expenses with the mechanic. He had to give us a sales slip and receipts when we bought supplies. And then no one could say anything to us. And we wrote down everything in a notebook, so they couldn't find a way to harm us.

There was, as I have mentioned, a little group that was composed of those who were in agreement with Gori, the man who was leader previously, because they believed that the government was going to give us the lots and that they would not have to pay anything to get all the services. And they even went to the newspaper to say that we were exploiting them, that all the money we collected for the water truck we were using to buy materials to build our house. But we had the majority of people on our side because they knew we told them everything though presenting them with the receipts.

Also during this time the municipal president ceded us the temporary use of a pick-up to collect garbage until such time as he could send someone who drove the municipal garbage trucks. He sent one after 3 or 4 months and since then the garbage collector has not failed us. During this time the municipal president was the engineer Guillermo Aldrete Has.

After awhile everything was supplied. We kept the water truck until we were certain that they were going to put in running water. Because to get this service we did have to put on a collective demonstration. We got together with a number of other *colonias populares*. Each *colonia* had its representative and each representative brought their petitions and also the people that supported them. But during this demonstration there were repressions from the municipal police. According to them we were making too much of an uproar on the civic center square, where all the powers—judicial, legislative, and executive—are concentrated. There the municipal palace is located as well, where the office of the civil registry and the office where we go to pay property taxes are located. And there you find the municipal president's office.

At that time two brothers—whose names I do not remember—were respectively chiefs of the judicial and the municipal police and they were who attacked us to the point that a pregnant woman miscarried. The chief of the municipal police commanded his policemen to dislodge us from the square. And since we did not leave, they began to hit the men and the men's wives got involved in defending them. And the pregnant woman told one of the policemen to stop hitting her husband, and he grabbed her by her arm and threw her on the ground, even though he saw what state she was in. She fell on her stomach and began to have very strong pains. But not even after that could they dislodge us.

And the governor's private secretary was in accordance with the police, saying that the men were going about drinking beer in the government center. And this was not true, because they closed the doors upon seeing that there were many of us in the square. And since at that time the governor was not in Mexicali, they invented many things.

We were between 300 and 400 persons. I told my people that they move away from the others and in case there was any repression, and that they remain silent. And that's what they did.

We stayed there for a week until the governor received us. Since he wasn't there we didn't leave. Well, we had to call him urgently and tell him that there was a demonstration and that we did not mean to leave until he met with us. Well, he had to come to Mexicali from Mexico City, because now we were getting out of order. And when he arrived he reunited all of the leaders, asking why they were making such a scandal. That it was not necessary to bring along so many people. That if a committee had presented itself, he would have received us. Well the secretary was in the audience with us, and we told him that it was a complete lie that they had been drinking because we didn't have enough money even to buy a taco, much less than buy a beer.

Indeed there were some comrades from other *colonias* that were a bit scandalous, but their leaders knew of them and warned them that if they were going to stage an uproar, better they leave. What I told my people was that they stay apart and if they saw anything or if someone did anything to them, that they tell me immediately.

But they were quiet, only displaying their cardboard signs that I had made for them, like "*Señor* governor, we want running water in our *colonia*, Unión de Residentes Lázaro Cárdenas," and "We are families with few resources, but we know how to pay." It is true that there were comrades from our *colonia* who didn't have a cent. We had to pay for their bus fare so that they could support us at the meetings and demonstrations. But with the money from the newspapers we sold we almost, almost financed all the costs. It was the only way they could show their support. And I made a great effort because I was lacking the same things as the other comrades. They had great trust in me. They said that whatever I proposed I carried out.

Well, I now knew how to handle things. If I became aggressive they were not going to listen to me. I arrived quietly, showing myself to be submissive and educated, even though I did not know how to use the words I spoke. But the governor understood me, and so I received more.

When he ordered us to come I went about organizing my people and someone told me he was awaiting me in his office. And the governor had the five leaders who had their people gathered in the square sitting in his office. I was the only one missing. But now they had opened the doors that overlooked the demonstration in front of the building, and the doors in the back, and I took advantage and had a person let me in. I was on the stairs to the second floor, when two policemen arrived and picked me up by my arms to throw me out, when a third policeman shouted that they should let me go up to the office where the others were meeting with the governor. And when I arrived he said to me, "Well where was my friend. We were waiting for you, to begin the discussion." And I felt tremendously embarrassed.

They had my chair ready for me. And he began talking, and he said, "You, Javier (nicknamed Pitufo), I now know what political party you belong to. Socorro, I already know you are a *priista* [member of the PRI political party, as was the governor]. You, Frederico, I also know what party you belong to. You, *doña* Gloria and Juana, I know what party you belong to also." And he failed to mention me. The truth is that that day I was very nervous because of what had happened before and also because he left me until last. Then he looked at me and said, "You, my friend, do you support the PRI?" I just nodded my head to say yes.

Well it was obvious that he knew me because he often saw me at the meetings when I took the people to our organization, the C.C.I. He always appeared there to support the people from the *ejidos*. They took us to the meetings like sheep. Thus it was that he was able to identify all who were leaders. The leaders refused to leave the governor's office. They went and demanded that they pay attention to them. Because of this he knew them. Because of this he believed what his secretary had told him about the uproar, about drinking beer. But I knew it hadn't happened and we refuted it there and then. Because Xico did indeed protest about this. And when we answered that all this was false, he turned to his secretary and said, "Now you see, secretary, that what

96

you told me was not true. You let yourself be led by what they told you without investigating. Well, *señores*, as regards why you came, each of you may explain your petitions." We were handing over the documents that each of us had brought. Then he told us, "I am going to check each notice. Come back in a week for an answer."

And each of us left. And the people were anxiously waiting for us outside and wanted us to tell them what had happened. And we told them what governor Xico had told us. And because of waiting, the people that were always with us, principally from our *colonia*, were thirsty and hungry. And we had to take turns with them in our houses and bring them tacos, even if they were just of beans. Those who didn't go to the demonstration aided us by sending food.

And I went and made a large pot of coffee for them to drink, and someone brought gallons of milk. Well, we mixed the coffee with a little milk, and assured that the children had a little glass of it. And we also bought loaves of bread. At this moment I didn't know if the other leaders took their people food or if they brought money to buy some, but I made sure for my people.

When the demonstration ended, we took away the utensils we had brought, like pots and frying pans, in which we had brought the food. There were comrades who didn't have even a cent, nor enough to buy a bus ticket. And Adolfo went around asking the bus passengers for a donation so as to pay the driver, and he received many. And as they gave Adolfo the coins, he gave them to the driver, and the driver was very content and thanked him.

It was a tremendous struggle having to deal with all kinds of people, whether in the *colonia* or in the government agencies, because there were secretaries there who were very inattentive. I was very patient and waited until they paid attention to the official papers I brought and that they signed them as received. But it was not just one office. I had to take copies to others.

I am always saying "I" but comrades (female) from the neighborhood committee also accompanied me. We were who worked hardest, because of our obligations to the community. They had to come to the place where I was selling newspapers and wait for me until I delivered the last newspaper, so I could leave. We were almost always three or four persons who worked harder than the other members of the committee.

This was one part of the struggle. Another one we had to confront was to come back to the *colonia* and gather the people together to inform them what we were doing and what advancements we had made as concerns the services like running water and sewerage. Because every service we wanted had to be asked for through petitions, because no government institution or developer had planned the *colonia*. It was an invasion, so everything was more difficult.

We also had to go to the nomenclature office so that they would give names to the streets, leaving a petition to request this. All of this we had to do. Later the called us in to ask us if we wanted to name the streets ourselves. And we took all the maps we had to the State Real Estate Office, which had given the plans to us. And so it was that the streets were named in honor of general Lázaro Cárdenas del Río. There was only one street that had the same name in a *colonia* called Lázaro Cárdenas, and ours was called Unión de Residentes Lázaro Cárdenas.

Well, we were looking for another name for this street, where we live, and it occurred to Adolfo that we name it Iztoc, after the oil well that caught on fire in the refinery. And I am writing down "the oil well" because I don't know what refinery or where it was because indeed I do not know much about geography, nor do I know where these oil wells that caught on fire back then are or were.

I answered Adolfo, "That's fine. Let's see if they accept it. Besides, our street is short, and the name as well." But when the came to hang the signs on the streets they had put "Ixtoc" with an "x" instead of a "z." And since they had already put them up we did not want to go and tell them that it was misspelled.

I forgot the most important thing for our children, the school that we had requested, and the kindergarten. We also had to go with our official documents to SEP [*Secretaría de Educación Pública*, Secretariat of Public Education] to submit petitions, and it was not very difficult there. We got a reply quickly. The land was registered immediately, first the kindergarten; the primary school took a little while longer. We had to build classrooms any way we could. The whole community cooperated to build then, even if it were out of old and cheap planks. But now we possessed a school. And when the teachers arrived to see what kind of school we had, they were enthusiastic about beginning with these children who lived in such precarious conditions. And up until now, 2016, there are teachers who have been there since back then. One teacher (male) who arrived to work in the school when elderly, now has retired. We had a celebration to pay homage to him. Another of the teachers is now principal, and two others continue teaching and are very nice people.

Now all of the classrooms are well built of solid materials. The municipal president ordered the construction of a shaded area made out of galvanized tin with a large courtyard, through the "*Escuela Digna*" program. And, well, the children are very happy.

Our first house in Unión de Residentes Lázaro Cardenas

First house, URLC, 1983

Tamar on roof in URLC, 1989

Daughter of Ernestina's *compadre* on the same street where she lives, 1990

Chapter 6. Union de Residentes Lazaro Cardenas II: Consolidation and Factionalism

Well, as I was relating in my account, there was also a tremendous struggle with another little group that formed. They were about 14 people who went to the newspaper office every once in awhile to say that I was exploiting them by asking them for money every week, up to 100 pesos, and because of this I was building a very big house. But, fortunately, the people know that I didn't ask them even for a cent. It was completely the opposite, because we paid for the copies of all the official papers that we presented from our own money. And the money for the house we were building came from the entire family's work vending newspapers. And it was fair that all of us should have dignified housing. They knew what work we did.

One time there was a reunion of many of the people from the *colonia*. A *señor* from the little group I mentioned said to me, in front of them all, that I was successful at the government agencies because I had sexual relations with everyone there. He said it more vulgarly than that, and the people wanted to lynch him. But I calmed them down and told them there was no reason to cause an uproar—that they return to their houses and I would sort this out with him. But the *señor* did not go home. He went into the house of one of the group, and I went to the salon of multiple uses to wait until he came out. I was waiting for him for almost two hours, along with one of my committee comrades (*doña* Josefina Soto). And when he came out I stopped him and demanded that he make me understand what he wanted to accomplish when he said all that foolishness in front of the people.

I was angry and going to give him a slap, but didn't since I saw he was carrying his little boy in his arms, like a shield, because he had seen I was waiting for him. By now it was about 9 at night. The meeting had ended at 7, and still he challenged me, saying, "How is it that by chance they listen to all you have to say?" And I said to him, "Let me know when I acted like a mattress, for you to say such a thing, or when you saw me leaving any hotel." With fury I told him to put the little boy down and to take his words back so I would rid myself of my anger. It wasn't so much anger for what he had said to me. After all, I knew it was not true. It was the way he said it to me in front of the people. And, yes, I got even with him by slapping him.

And my friend was going to hit him with a rock. It's just that I shouted to her not to do it, because it was not worth dirtying one's hands with a character such as this man, who was worse than a woman. And with every slap I gave him I said, this is for the old lady that you are, and this is for what you said in front of the people, and this one so that you remember me the rest of your life, you old gossip. My friend, very angry, shouted at him that, "What happened is that you have always resented Ernestina because she has ignored your insinuations. You are a whore in pants. You believe all women are as low as you are and you are mistaken."

Well, we didn't give him time to defend himself. I myself picked up his little boy and gave him to him, because the poor child had started to cry from fear. He was scarcely two yeas old and was stammering words that because of my anger I did not understand.

Well to keep going. Another day I went to the store and the first thing I see is the guy. And he spoke to me. I, with the fear that he was going to hurt me, went to the other side of the street, and there he stopped in front of me. He apologized to me and even said, "Ernestina, I assure you that never has a woman slapped me. You are the only one, and my respect goes to you. You are a very brave woman and I want you and I to be friends. I will never again say such stupid things. I want you to pardon me."

I forgave the *señor* but I didn't pardon him because only God can pardon. "But I want you, since you said this foolishness in front of the people, I want you to ask my forgiveness in front of them."

"Of course I am in agreement and I know that I have tried to be more than friendly with you and you have rejected me, as well. You have never been like other women."

"Look, *señor*, I have my dignity and will always have it, but we are not talking about that. I believe you are in agreement with what I have proposed. I hope that when we have a neighborhood meeting you will come and ask for forgiveness, because it is not only to me that you owe you apologies—even if you don't belong to this *colonia*, because your house is outside the boundaries of it. But take into account that I can help you to get the same services as us. It is all a question of how you behave with us, and you will see that you will be benefited. You are a good person but have come under the bad influence of other people, and you know whom I am referring to.

Well, to cut the story short, I told this *señor* where he had to go to solicit services such as running water, sewerage, and electricity. Because he had been getting water from a little canal for almost 40 years. He had a septic tank for the toilet and lit his house with candles. Well, now he has everything we do.

There were other cases like this one. Another *señora*, elderly—she could hardly walk, but she liked to do harm. She said we couldn't do anything to her because she had good contacts in the PRI. And since she transported people to the campaigns she was in tight with the government officials. This *señora* was about 90 years old but she still felt strong even though they had to help her to board the buses. She was blind. She walked with a cane in order to know where she was stepping. But the same was as that *señor*, she made life difficult for me. She said things to me on the street. She couldn't see but she could recognize voices. When I saw her on the street I had to pass by her without making any noise. And if I passed by and someone greeted me and mentioned my name, careful Ernestina! Because she said things, even that I was going to die. But I no longer took her into account. It was a daily occurrence.

This didn't make me lose sleep, because I had other things to think about and to put in order—my ideas as to how not to commit errors in front of the government officials, and how to touch their cold hearts—because all of them thought either politically or technically. So I had to bring the other me and convince them of what I stood for. Not just to ask them that they go to put in running water, or sewerage, or whatever was needed. No! I had to engage their humanitarian side and this was my goal. Not listening to little groups who wanted to continue living their entire lives without it costing them anything.

Because in the moment we wanted to have a patrimony, we had to pay a tribute to the government—pay taxes—because all the soil we walk upon we are paying for and we must be conscious of it. From the time our parents take us to register our births, one is paying the government a registration fee to make us citizens and have us on their list. That is the way it is with everything and those who say they don't want to pay are finished and don't know what a responsibility or an obligation is. And we had to pay for the lots and the services they would put in the *colonia*.

Another situation that happened to me was when the State Real Estate Office made a map of the *colonia*. When they gave me a copy of it, block number 1 had 13

105

unoccupied lots, and I hadn't known about it. But since I had a list of those asking for lots, I went and asked the architect (female) and engineer (male) what they were going to do with this block. And they answered that they indeed had a list of people to put in there.

Well I, neither late nor lazy, had already put a family in each lot. But I never asked the office anything in writing to prove the existence of the families who had entered. And so it happened that about a month later, a man appeared who according to these families seemed to be a policeman. He brought a notebook and asked them their names and also asked each one of them who had let them enter here. Well they, with no fear, gave my name. And I had even told them, "You continue living here. No one is going to throw you out, because this block is part of the *colonia*." And that is how things were. It had not even occurred to me to go to the State Real Estate Office.

When I arrived from work, I put down the newspapers that remained, and gathered together my children's clothing—dirty from selling newspapers—so they could go to school in their uniforms. When I was washing the clothes in the canal I went into the water fully clothed and scrubbed the dirty clothing on a rock, when a car arrived and parked where I was. The *señor* who got out of the car asked my name. And he showed me some sheets of paper and asked me, "Do you know what this is?" And I answered him affirmatively. For this they brought a policewoman. "It is a warrant for arrest. But we are not going to take you in. It is only to conduct an investigation."

And I answered, "That's fine. Just let me change my clothing, because it is wet. Take me to my house, so I can change."

But they answered me, "It is not necessary. We are going to return soon."

"Then let me pass by the house and tell my family that you are taking me."

"That's fine. We are going to pass by."

The only person in the house was my eldest daughter, *la gorda*. And I managed to tell her that the police were taking me to the police station. My daughter began to cry, feeling impotent because she could not do anything. And she immediately went and told the neighborhood committee members and they went and told everyone that they should go to the jail, because the police had detained me. Then Adolfo arrived. They told them they had brought a list of other comrades who were working, and that they would pass by for them. Someone let these comrades know, and they were able to attend.

Thus, when we arrived at the jail, almost everyone from the *colonia* was waiting. When they saw that they took me out of the car all wet, the people became furious and began to shout. It's just that Adolfo quieted them down. He told him that one gained nothing by shouting, and that they would take part in saying what was just about what they were doing with the president and the other comrades.

At this moment they took me and the other comrade, and after awhile the police went for the other two women that were missing. We were only four. I never knew or wanted to ask why. Well, they booked and processed up within the hour. But they didn't take into account that people from the C.C.I. worked in the police department. And I told the director of the prison to treat us well and not put us together with the other prisoners. That they give us good treatment and let the people give us covers and food until everything was taken care of. Because we were not criminals and it had been an error on the part of the State Real Estate Office for having assigned lands that did not belong to the *colonia*.

And they arrested the other two comrades when the police arrived at their houses to bring them in. And the police did the same to them as they had done to me and to my comrade. But this gave me greater strength to continue on, even though the people said that when I was taken out to testify, I should resign. But I told them, "These comrades are motivating me even more. Don't worry, I am going to get out soon."

Angelina Solorio was protecting me. Because they even put me in a cell that had a shower and a bed and also a toilet, and was occupied by two prisoners. But they were not dangerous. One of them lent me a dress, because I had arrived all wet. I got tonsillitis there. I was in jail for 24 hours. Even though it was not a lot of the time, the people from the *colonia* were present all afternoon and night until Adolfo, my husband could go to the C.C.I. and get a lawyer who would come to defend us.

Well, that's what happened. All four of us got out because of lack of proof. But indeed Adolfo had to pay bail for all of us, 80 pesos each one. And we had to sign in at the police department every week for two months. But later I told the judge that I was going to go to visit my daughters who were in the teachers' training school in Chihuahua and he answered me that I would not have any problems if I went and didn't come to sign in. And he gave me a paper saying that I no longer had obligations.

But I wanted to make sure it was not a trap, and I went to consult a lawyer from the C.E.S.P.M. (*Comisión Estatal de Servicios Públicas de Mexicali*. Mexicali State Commission of Public Services). And he advised me to retain him as my personal lawyer and that he would investigate with judge number 3 of the prison. So it was.

I still have the papers naming him as my lawyer. And later he asked me to come in and commented that all was in order and that I could go to see my daughters.

It was a very precarious situation, because for going around like the mother of charity, many things happened to me. Everything happened. When I sent to the State Real Estate Office, I told them what had happened. They went to see the land and, in effect, they had mapped it incorrectly and they had to move the people to the empty lots that existed in the *colonia*, and some were still unoccupied. Well out of this sprung another problem. Since I was going around with the social worker and the people saw me with her, they went and told the owners of the lots, and the lot owners went to defend them. But it was no longer valid, because the list of possessors had been finalized. The blamed me for putting the new petitioners in their lots. But it was the decision of the State Real Estate Office.

One of the people had not contracted her lot, nor lived on it. She came and complained to me and, well, I told her that she knew where to go to lodge a complaint. She went to the leader of another *colonia*. Both came when I was there, at the Real Estate Office, and the leader was very angry and very aggressive. But since she saw me, she came directly to me and protested because I had taken away the *señora*'s lot. And she wanted to throw me off the second floor's balcony.

I felt that everything had ended for me. I became more nervous than when the police had taken me from the canal to the jail. If the workers from the State Real Estate Office had not come to my rescue I would have died on the floor below. I thank God and these workers that I am still alive today.

These have been some of my experiences. I decided my goal would be to remain until we got all the services. The only thing that took a long time was the land titles and the pavement. They did not give us titles until 2012. I am talking since 1985, the year we contracted the lots and stopped being only possessors. When we contracted we pledged to pay for the land within three years and the document guaranteed that we were owners. Even though we didn't have titles, no one could remove us.

So I remained president of the *colonia* until 1992. By then I was tired of so many problems. I decided to leave them in charge of someone else. I called together the whole community to announce my resignation. And even though they did not want to accept it, my decision was categorical. It was the day before my birthday, November 7th. And the following day, my comrades gathered to talk to me. It was about 7 at night, and I asked myself what they wanted now.

A *señora* came to my house and said, "Ernestina, get ready, because there are some government officials in the salon and they wish to talk to you urgently. They are very elegantly dressed, so make yourself attractive." At that moment I was very disheveled. And the *señora* said to me, "I'll wait while you change clothes. You are not going like that, are you?"

"Of course not." Adolfo had bought me a dress that looked like a Christmas tree, for occasions such as this. I remember it was black, but it looked very ridiculous to me, because it had sequin flowers, and I thought it quite ugly. But I had no other option.

Well, I went, after getting ready with my dress and high-heeled shoes, very elegant, according to me. And I said to the *señora*, "Where are the people and the politicians?" And I was surprised when she answered me that they were inside the salon. The lights were off. Well, probably they were tired of waiting and had gone away. But she opened the door and switched on the lights. Everyone in the *colonia* was there, and they were waiting for me. They had fixed up the salon and began to sing me *las mañanitas* [the traditional Mexican happy birthday song]. Well, among them all, each one had donated to give me a farewell party and chose my birthday.

There was a *señor* who had a *sonido* (sound machine with loud speakers, to play cassettes) and offered to bring it. And, well, I began to cry. And well, they brought me gifts and threw a party there. They said they were grateful for my having helped them with anything that came up. We dined and we danced, and well, I also thanked them for having given me their support. And I told them, "Without you I wouldn't have been able to do anything even if I had wanted to. Because for these things it is necessary to work as a team and you were an excellent team. Through good times and bad times, you were with me."

I reminded them of all we had done and of when ex-president Salinas de Gortarí presented himself to us. That I had not known what clothing to wear because supposedly I was going to enter by his side, because he had chosen me as one of the most honest of *colonia* leaders. And a neighbor who worked collecting recyclables from the municipal dump—he collected clothing that was sometimes even ironed as well—and he said to me, "Come, I have something for you to put on." And so it was. I dressed in clothing from the dump and he said to me, "No one will know from where you got this very elegant clothing." So I dressed and presented myself and was by the side of Salinas de Gortarí and the Secretary of Military Defense. And at this moment, I felt like a very important person.

Well, I was giving you all my anecdotes because not everyone knows how I spent my days in the offices of the agencies. It was not easy, but look, *señores*, at the result of our struggle. I did not tell these things so they would feel sorry for me, but simply that they became conscious of all they did for themselves. And it was not easy to take away their homes.

Of course there were some who as soon as they contracted their lots they sold them and left and then later returned to ask me for a lot. And I sent them packing and they got a bad impression of me and joined the other little group to see if they could obtain something. But the little opposition group had no power, because they were not registered as a committee.

This little group was only validated in politics through carting people to the campaigns or meetings held by the PRI party. They wanted to stage a revolution in the *colonia* through wheeling and dealing, so that we could not function or do our social work.

I was one of those people who didn't like to fight with others, even less so knowing the conditions under which they lived. The committee that we formed was only and exclusively aimed at getting services for the *colonia* Unión de Residentes. And it is true that once in a while the party asked us to gather the people together and invited us to some meeting they were having. But this was up to each resident. They were not obliged to go and much less in exchange for something. Everything was voluntary. And since the people knew our committee was strong, they showed up for us. Of course we too were affiliated with the PRI, but without any obligations. And we told our people clearly that their IFE credential specified no particular political party affiliation. They could vote for whomever they pleased. They were not obligated to do anything. It was just that when we went to any government agency, if the functionaries asked us what political party we belonged to, we said the PRI, so that they would take good and rapid care of us. But we had this goal.

The people knew all this. It was unnecessary to repeat it again and again. And this angered the little group that was our enemy. The president of this faction was a very conflictive person.

And I, as the *colonia* representative, did not allow her to meddle in my affairs, because it would make everything more difficult. But there was no distinction between us, because all the work that we accomplished was for the whole community. In the end it was for the benefit of all, enemies or not. The party took her items of food to dispense for her family and her little group, which was composed of not even 15 members. They were never going to compete with the majority of the *colonia*.

Meanwhile, a message was sent to my house saying that a large truck had been detained at the customs with items of food for the *colonia*, but that it was necessary for us to go and tell the customs officials that it was for us to share, and thus they would let it pass. And when the truck arrived, the people were lined up and orderly, waiting to receive the food. I am not talking about a small truck. It was a trailer truck from the U.S., though I don't know what organization sent it. They came several times to distribute food items and toys for the children. They even distributed bicycles to the youngsters. This was about 1986.

Then this *señora* was so angry. The strange thing is that whenever we met, we greeted one another as though we were good friends. But we did not get together for any community activities. Over this we indeed clashed. Then she even told a woman that she would pay her two thousand *pesos* if she beat me up. It´s just that the woman opposed it, saying why was she going to beat me up if I hadn't done anything to her. And I found out about this because she told me, "Ernestina, those two thousand *pesos* were very tempting to me then. I wanted to go and beat you up, but I said to myself, how am I going to beat her up if she hasn't even done anything to me? I would have been crazy to face you and say *doña* Toña sent me to fight with you and beat you up." That was the name of the president of the other faction, *doña* Toña.

"Then why didn't she come to my house to beat me up, if she wanted to so much?"

" Ah, because she is not a fool. She wanted to compromise me and then wash her hands of it, claiming that she had not sent me to beat you up."

"If as you say this two thousand *pesos* were very tempting and you were very poor, you should have come on and beat me. But let's see who would have won. Me. I was not going to give up even if I was losing. But neither am I going to lower myself to fight, because it is not a question of doing this even if we do not get along."

And everything was for the good of everyone. What we were going about doing did not hurt anyone. To the contrary, it was about making them content. But instead of naming the *colonia Unión* de Residentes, it should have been called *Disunión* de Residentes. Do you believe that it was fun or not wearing me down to go around carrying documents to state and municipal government agencies and that at times to go about without eating so that the offices would accept the documents so I could bring back good news? Of course the majority were awaiting news that was convenient for them. No, friend, it was convenient for me more than for all of you that they respond to me so that I could come and share the news with you. At times I didn't have enough money for even a soda. I say soda, but not even for a glass of water.

None of these people knew, and if I told them, what was I going to gain? Yes, there were times that in order for the people to accompany us we had to pay for their bus tickets. And I was not going to be so insensitive or thoughtless as to ask money from them. I preferred to endure until I got home. It is true that they waited for me all day, outside the offices, until I got a good response.

It also cost me a great deal of effort to win the trust of some of the families who had supported the previous "president" of the colonia. But in the end I won their support. Everything was a question of persevering until they accepted me. They almost never attended the meetings of the neighborhood committee when we invited them to. They did not decline but neither did they come. Until little by little they drew closer to us, because we didn't go around telling them lies.

And if the personnel did not respond well in one office, we also put an announcement in the stores about what they had said. And we convoked a neighborhood meeting to say that we must stage a peaceful protest in accordance with the subject we were dealing with. And that's what we did. We went in little by little until the offices were filled up and they would thus pay attention to us. Then they asked us who was the representative of the group, and the people told them I was. But they wanted only the neighborhood committee to come in. But I told them I had not brought the people along just so they would accompany me. They want to hear everything that is said and reach an agreement in case we were denied whatever the subject was that we were treating. Fortunately, all of the people were let in. There were many protests.

All that I was handling so they would pay attention and wait on us was not only for my personal benefit, it was for the whole community. My goal was that we all would have the indispensable services. Not just necessary. They were indispensable. Like running water, electricity, and sewerage. And later the services that were not so urgent would come along.

When they named me, in 1985, the representative of the *colonia*, I promised them that the first thing I was going to apply for was electricity. Because seeing that so many households were burning manure to keep the mosquitos away, there was much contamination in the environment. And the children were smelling of burnt manure, and all black from the smoke, besides the effect on their lungs. Their lungs could be filled up with all the smoke they inhaled. And with electricity they could have a fan to take away the heat and blow the mosquitos away.

The running water, so they could take a bath, wash dishes, and their clothing with clean water. Even though there was an irrigation canal on two sides of the *colonia* the water was very contaminated because of all the garbage that people were throwing in it. There were times that the children went swimming in the canal to overcome the heat. Pimples broke out all over their bodies, because people didn't just throw garbage in the canal, but even dead animals. And it was no longer convenient to have the canal. Mosquitos bred in it. And furthermore, it was used as drainage for the leftover chemicals from the factories.

Sewerage was also indispensable for us, because with it one could have their own toilet inside the house, instead of building outhouses. And also the environment would not be so contaminated by bad smells and one would not have to go about digging holes all over the yard [for successive outhouses], and everyone would have their own plumbing. We realized all of these dreams, along with the contracting of our properties, the naming of the streets, the primary school, the fence around the primary school, the kindergarten, and all that came besides this.

The salon of multiple uses—now the Catholic Church—was also built, and also the little park for children's games. A charitable group economically supported the building of the salon of multiple uses. I don't remember very well but I think the group was named "*Los Vecinos*" ["The Neighbors", a Los-Angeles based charitable organization]. And we were six persons that they gave keys to the salon, so we would have a place for neighbors' meetings. We also had dances there, with the aid of the community. A sound machine would be contracted and the youngsters showed up to dance.

But some time later the problems with the little group began again. They claimed to be very Catholic and they took over the salon and turned it into a church. They began to bring in things that would be useful in a church. And so the dances ended. They said the salon was serving only for things of the devil, like the dances, for example. And we didn't want to argue the point. The neighborhood committee withdrew from the topic once and for all, because the priests began to interfere as well. And we opted to leave the salon in the interests of maintaining peace, and now it is a church.

And everything began changing and I announced that I was going to retire from the neighborhood committee, that I resigned, and that it was now time for another person to continue on as representative. But no one wanted the responsibility. And I gave them a long time for someone to say that s/he was ready to take on the obligation.

It's that it was not easy going around confronting people who at times did not want to attend to you, and waiting all day for them to deal with the official papers, and presenting petitions for what was needed, so that the day would be fruitful, and going to talk to the people about what had been achieved. And all these efforts without eating and being treated as though we were begging for alms. (Of course, luckily, they waited on me and gave me good responses, because I was perseverant). So it was logical that no one wanted to take responsibility for anything.

I remained still longer because they asked me to. "Comrades," thus I said to the *señores* and *señoras*, and that is how we treated each other, as comrades. It was very nice when we all got together to talk. When we met in the street we greeted each other with much respect. There was a *señor* from Oaxaca that as soon as he saw me, even from afar, shouted, "*señora* president," or he said "my president." He'd run over and greet me with much respect and happiness and say, "No, my president, the day you resign it is not going to be the same. And the *colonia* will remain as it is. There will be no one who wants to assume the responsibility. And remember what I tell you, that is the way it will be."

I said to him, "You take a chance, and we all will help you, you will see."

"No, my president, imagine the mistakes I am going to make since I don't know how to read or write. I don't even know how to write my name. When I sign important papers I have to put my fingerprint or a cross on them."

"But you know how to express yourself very well and for this it is not necessary to read or write. That's why there is a committee, so the secretary will write down what you dictate."

"No, my president. What happens if I dictate something and they do not write it down and when I go in to deliver some documents they laugh at me because it says something else?"

"No, comrade, give it to another person who knows how to read before you go to deliver it and you will erase your doubts. So you must take a risk an accept, for as they say, he who doesn't risk something does not win something."

"No. Why do you believe the other comrades are going to accept me—because I am a poor illiterate."

"Because you know how to defend yourself very well and without using curse words. Well then, what do you say? Will you come forward to take over the post as the president of the *colonia*? Because if we let others eat our bread, we are going to be sorry."

"Look, my president, call together another meeting of the neighbors and ask again who wants to take on the responsibility of moving forward to represent the *colonia*, and if you find any candidate, mention it. And if that person doesn't want to do it, I will come forward. What do you think? Is that alright?"

"It seems good to me."

I again called together a meeting to advise that if they couldn't find another candidate, well I was going to resign in any case, because my goals had been achieved. Well the candidate I had chosen was there, hiding so I would not see him. And I said to them, "Look among you for someone you can trust and who is willing to work hard for the *colonia*." Well, they called forward about seven people. But no one wanted to take charge. They came forward with embarrassment, but they came forward. And I called the *señor* (give him whatever name you wish), but he had repented about what he had said.

But the people were voting for all of them, and some definitively did not want the post, and they withdrew. And I said to this *señor*, "Well, will you then come forward?"

And he answered me, "Look, my president, if the comrades elect me, I will accept, but meanwhile you must look for someone else. I must tell you up front that I know neither how to read nor write. So you are taking a risk with me. I will accept, but as I said, only until you find another candidate, and with the promise that you help me write up those papers you take to the civic center. And when you are going to deliver them, be very careful about what you tell me, and what you are going to deliver—because you of the committee know how to read and write. And what do you say, yes or no?"

Well, he got everyone on his side because of what he said, and everyone applauded. So the change of president was effected.

But this *señor* did not last long, maybe seven months. And he wanted to quit because he said that he could not bear the burden—that it was very difficult because he lost a lot of time going around and around, and who was going to support his family? "I work to support my family or to go around as a troublemaker. I don't say my president was going around as that, because wherever she went they took her into account. And they asked me about her. They spoke very well of her. On that side I became disillusioned about many things the other leaders were doing, just exploiting people and asking them for money. I heard some *señoras* talking and they said they were asked for 100 pesos every week, and if they wanted more money they went around asking for contributions. And one of the *señoras* said, 'I couldn't give him any more than 30 pesos. I had nothing more.' And the other said, 'Well, I didn't give him anything and such as it is, I am not going to give him anything, because he is an exploiter.' And my president never has asked even a cent of us. If she went to make copies, it was from her own pocket. Or tell me if one day she asked any of you for anything, and how much it was. I myself saw how the whole family got up early to go to work, and how she moved the *colonia* forward. And meanwhile, I am resigning because you know that this responsibility is not easy."

Because of this they stood quietly. There were no comrades who could participate or and no comrade who would raise her hand and say, "I can do it." And I told them, "I would wish that one of you would take on this burden because I well know that without any leader, other leaders who are not from here are going to want to take over and then, for certain they will ask us for donations. And I don't say 10 or 20 pesos. They are going to ask us for 100 pesos or more."

Well, no one wanted the responsibility, and the *colonia* remained without anyone to take charge. I withdrew from any compromises but comrades still came by and I helped them to resolve the problems that they had concerning their property. And I did it without asking anything in return. I guided them as to the offices they had to go to, and if some person could not do it, I took on the responsibility of accompanying her. But now it was not the same as being obligated to everyone. It was a private matter and they were isolated cases.

Everything was very different. I remember when they wanted to invade a lot that had been set aside for a medical clinic, this near the primary school. I still have the documents concerning the contract. I had to go a remove this family and they had no need to inhabit it, they were just little guinea pigs for the infamous president (female) of PRI who wanted this lot in order to put in other people. And she contracted with them so they would invade. The good thing is that some people advised me quickly and brought me the documents to show the family. And I warned them that if they did not get out I was going to send for a patrol car to remove them. That it should not occur to them to put up even one rail for construction.

That was when I found out that they were protecting this *señora*. Well, this *señora* and the people who supported her were going to go to the Public Ministry

(*Ministerio Público*). I, very brave according to myself, confronted them and I thought, what if they grab me and beat me, and I who came alone. Even that could happen, if they were not reluctant to do so.

Then they took away their things and afterwards I went to verify that they had left. Well, there was nobody there. I no longer wanted to be bothered with these things. But I was not going to let people invade this lot if it was already set apart for something good for the community. Later a medical clinic opened on that lot, but nobody went there, so afterwards they closed it.

As for others who invaded the green area [small park, on the street where the primary school is], it was not as important to me, because there was no document protecting it. It just appeared on the map of the *colonia*, and if the State Real Estate Office did nothing to kick them out, well, let them stay. And they had electricity, running water, and sewerage, but they were irregular lots. They had neither contracts nor titles, and if that did not bother them, there was no problem. The only thing is that, disagreeably, there is where the majority of drug addicts live. Those who pass by are at risk of being assaulted so the addicts can rob the little that they have with them, and of being offered drugs. But it is each one's affair, whether they buy drugs or not.

And the only thing is when my grandchildren and my daughter—who live in the neighboring *colonia* Satélite—pass by there, I tell them to very careful. That they pay attention to whoever approaches them to say something to them or to offer them drugs. But since I know everyone who lives there and they know my family, they do not get involved with us. Just the opposite, we pass by and they greet us nicely, and I feel secure when I see them sitting in the little park and they call to me and wave.

This area is indeed very risky, because various people have been assaulted. But they are people the addicts don't know. And bicycle riders have been beaten up and robbed. It is on a street that has a bridge built on top of large tubes so that pedestrians can pass, not so cars can pass. But now it has become customary for cars to drive over it. And they do not respect the people who are walking. They almost knock them into the drain. It is a drain or canal for chemical wastes, as I mentioned. It is a high risk to people both because of the passing cars and because of the danger of being assaulted while walking. But I can't get involved in this, because it is an affair for the police.

Dead bodies have been found beside the tubes. It is not known if they have been thrown there or what has happened. Because they have been found wrapped up in blankets and tied up but with nothing stolen. I mean they have all their personal documents.

Before it was like a small arroyo, and the municipal government filled it in, and converted it into a canal. It was because of the committee, that I agreed with, that we ordered the installation of these two large tubes with the goal that the children of both *colonias*—Satélite and our colonia, could cross. Because the secondary school is located in the *colonia* Satélite, near the aforementioned canal, and the primary school in our *colonia* is also close by it, we opted for the time being to have a passage-way between the two *colonias*. But since they paved this street on both sides, that of Satélite and our *colonia*, without taking into account the consequences, it stayed that way. And when the students are going to pass over the bridge, and a car is coming, they have to stop and wait until it crosses because the road over the canal is so narrow that they could be hit. The water is very contaminated. Dogs have fallen in, and they come out without hair. But the authorities have neglected to respond to our concerns.

All this I did after resigning from the neighborhood committee. But I have been unable to break away. Even though much time has passed, people continue to come to my house and I tell them how to obtain titles for their property. Because acquiring the titles came to us very late. And since the representative of the State Real Estate Office came and advised me—this was in 2012—that now the people could come in for their property titles, I had to put up signs in the few stores, so that people would know to go to retrieve them. I do not know if they have gone or if they expect me to bring them the titles. I fulfilled my obligation by posting the message. And I am not going to take them the titles because they have to pay, a very low sum, but it must be paid.

And for the people who present their pensioner's credential, or who are elderly, the titles are free. Like I did not pay even a cent for my title because I presented my over-60 credential. Previously we had only a buyer-seller contract with the state government. But this meant we had to pay property taxes, and no one could take our house lots away. And besides, the majority of us have upgraded our houses with solid materials, like bricks and cement blocks.
Now I can say that it is totally mine.

Back then when I began with the neighborhood committee, I was 35 years old and it was when we contracted for the residential lots. And when I later went to pick up my property title, it was 27 years later, when I was 62. By then I had my over-60 credential, INAPAM (*Instituto Nacional de Adultos Mayores*, National Institute for Elderly Adults).

There were people who never got to see their titles, because they had died. And in the worse case they died without a will and their offspring were unable to change the ownership name because they fought among themselves. They could not reach an agreement as to who would be chosen to inherit the property. They have come to my house so that I would counsel them and what I could tell them was that all of them should reach an agreement and write a letter showing that they agreed as to the name of the person that was going to be the owner, and present themselves at a notary's office.

Because, as a matter of fact, it was necessary for someone to be named as owner. Or simply that it remain in the same owner's name while they continued paying property taxes and if they did not do this it could be transferred to the municipality which could lay an embargo on it, and it would be very difficult to get back. "You yourselves have to resolve this. The only thing I can advise you is that you gather together the necessary documents concerning the piece of land and your birth certificates together with your identifications and go to the notary or simply to the State Real Estate Office, to see what they counsel you."

That was all I could do to help. There are cases that I feel sorry to reject, but now I do not want to, or cannot go around and around because my economic situation no longer lets me—apart from the fact that I no longer have the time to be mixed up in things. My time is very limited. Now I am programmed like robots.

Because of this I tried to make them understand that they should look for someone else to help them out. But they didn't want to. Yes, there were other people who came and offered them aid, but of another kind, like bringing food items, noting down their names for their over 60 credentials, helping them with construction materials. Including distributing high definition televisions to the majority after the infamous change from analogic programming, so they had no need to buy the famous de-codifiers. The televisions were distributed under the program, *Tarjetas sin Hambre*, part of the *Prospera* program that replaced *Opportunidades*, and also gave them food items every Christmas. [*Prospera*, the name given to the conditional cash transfer program under Peña Nieto, replaced *Opportunidades*, but also amplified the benefits.]

But there was no one to advise them on other subjects, advice they really needed. Of course all is good when they have someone who gives these things, but these same persons who go to offer help with all these things I mentioned, could counsel them. But if no one tells them, they are not going to know the situation of each and every family.

There is also a program that reaches many families called *Oportunidades* [now called *Prospera*], distributing money for the children's school uniforms . And what they do, at times they go and spend it, and don't even buy a uniform for their children. The children go to school with a uniform faded from so much washing and their shirts ripped. I say this because I have seen children go to school in this condition. Because of this at times I get angry that their mothers put on a suffering act. And I have seen how they bring them materials for their houses, and afterwards they go about selling it, as they do the food items (like coffee, flour, rice, cooking oil, beans, pastas, cans of tuna fish and sardines). Even if they have to go to the civic center to collect the items it is the same. After awhile they go around selling them and it is by the box-load that they distribute the provisions. They are worth two thousand *pesos* every month, and ten thousand *pesos* for the building materials.

All this does not seem just to me, and I comment on it because people have arrived shamelessly to my house to sell me building materials—like laminas, cement, rolls of cyclonic fencing. And food items as well. It is just that I refuse to buy from the people who come and offer me these goods, because I know where they come from. I would have wished to have had this help at the beginning. I would have been able to build a better house without the need for buying all the materials. Even so, I was criticized a lot. When we began to build the walls of the house that we have today, some contrary people said that the house came from all the money the water truck was earning. They didn't pay attention to what they were saying and did so without seeing how the whole family were killing ourselves selling newspapers in all weather and at the crossroads. But, well, it remains with me only as a memory.

For me it was a very difficult epoch: having to go to sell newspapers and from there move on to deliver documents to distinct government agencies. Perhaps the people of my *colonia* don't remember this. Or perhaps one *señora* or another starts talking about how they suffered in order to acquire a piece of land for the welfare of their children. Above all, because it is not the same to be paying rent in a complex of apartments for something that will never be theirs, or living in a borrowed house. Moreover, I didn't ever dream of having my own house. And less so, given our economic neediness.

But the opportunity to invade presented itself, and we established ourselves. And so with many families who still live on their lots, because others left as soon as they were contracted. I never saw them again. Maybe they did not like the place, or maybe they had a better opportunity. I don't know, but I am very happy that the families who previously lived on the brickyards stayed here and that some of their children were born here in the *colonia*, and that their school-age children were able to study. Now some of their children's children go to high school and some even to the university.

Of course not all went on to higher schooling. Because perhaps they did not have the opportunity—their economic level did not permit them to. And maybe because they did not want to finish their studies in order to have a better life. But others have been happy. Now married and working in the maquiladoras they have their little houses, gotten with the aid of the program they have for employees and which they take out of the payroll (INFONAVIT).

There are other youngsters that are on the tip of finishing their university education. All these youngsters—grandchildren of the brickmakers, whose children worked with them on the brickyards—have a solid goal and do not want to be like their grandparents or parents, mixing the clay and doing humiliating work. All work is of value and honest as long as it is not prohibited by law. And may they be grateful to their parents. Because since they have worked with effort to bring them up, their children and grandchildren should not be ashamed of them. Thee are youngsters who did not continue studying beyond secondary school. They later married but they have a good job like being contractors for big construction projects involving metal and drywall structures in plazas, factories, and other social centers. And they also have their workers, electricians, plumbers. That way they and their workers earn a salary above minimum wage.

And while there is this type of family, there are others who prefer to go to work in the United States and thus were not taking care of their adolescent children. Most care has to be taken at this age. Because they are youngsters that anyone can involve or trap into their illegal transactions or they are simply victims of drugs. First the traffickers let them try the drugs for free and afterward they are tempted and cannot break away from them. That is what happens when they become addicts to the vice. And it is they who go about robbing in order to obtain money to continue using drugs. And all this is because people are not paying attention to what their children are doing.

I do not say that mine are little white doves, but I pay attention to how they come home. Because immediately one know what state they are in, because one notices if they are drunk or drugged. And so I can affirm that there are many standards of living among the families who reside in the colonia. Including dysfunctional families where the papa and mama are constantly fighting in front of their offspring, and each one goes his or her own way.

When friends of my children arrived at my house—they had almost no friends but the few that they had—I myself invited them in. But I was always watching them to see what activities they engaged in. They played the music of their era, music that they liked. Nor am I going to say music of my era, because it seemed boring to them, but of rock and roll groups. But I did like their coming and even spent some time talking with them. They brought their little cans of beer, but asked me permission first. And so that they would be in my house and didn't go drinking elsewhere, I gave them permission. And they even invited me for a glass and I accepted with pleasure. But also so they would feel comfortable.

And they even called me "chief" (*jefa*)—because I was chief of the tribe. And up until today they continue calling me chief. All are now married but they continue to visit. And some are living abroad, but they still meet up, and, well, I receive them with great pleasure, and also because their mamas are my friends. We, the mamas, talk on the telephone and they visit me. We sit and remember many things and laugh about all we have lived through all these years.

It is also nice to remember the moments we were in agreement when a problem arose, and how we helped one another. And when Mother's Day neared, we came to an agreement to ask for donations from the establishments in order to celebrate the 10th of May. The stores gave us food items, and the maquiladoras gave us money. There was an owner of a ranch where cattle were raised, not far from the colonia. He told us, "I will donate the chicken. Just tell me how many boxes you need, and I will buy them."

"Well, whatever you wish, nothing more. Just note that we are about 100 mothers, apart from the people who we are inviting because they were nice enough to give us a donation."

"That's fine. You can count on seven boxes. How does that seem?"

"Of course that seems perfect. Well, many thanks, *señor*."

"I am here to help you out with whatever I can. You know you can count on me. And I will be there with my wife, and if my daughters-in-law wish to go, we will bring them. Is that alright?"

"Of course. We count on your being there. It would be an honor."

That is the way we worked in the beginning. We had our get together with what the others bought. The only thing lacking was holding a dance. And the place where we got together was a large site that served as a workshop. They owner lent it to us whenever we needed it—because by then the salon was a church. At this time we also had the *quinceañeras* (15 year old girls) for whom I was godmother. And I was godmother for about seven other 15-year-old girls. Perhaps out of gratitude or perhaps because they really wanted me to be one of their godmothers.

And my friends and I remembered so many things. We shed tears of emotion. And they said to me, "Listen, Ernestina, when will we have another party so that we can get together and pass some time with pleasure? But only with people who helped us in the moments we needed it."

"Whenever you like. You know that I am happy to go partying and ready to party as well. Just let me know in time. The good thing is that we now have an apparatus to play music. Here are my jukeboxes. So don't cry." And we would sing or howl like wolves.

It is very nice when you walk along with your head held high, without fear of aggression, even verbal. Quite the opposite, I can go out to the street and everyone has greeted me with respect. At times I go out at 10 at night to buy something for an early breakfast, and I go out with great confidence because I know that nothing will happen to me, even with the little groups smoking marijuana. But this doesn't scare me because I know they are trustworthy and if anything untoward should happen to me, I know they will protect me.

Like they once did when some gang members from the nearby *colonia* (Satélite) wanted to assault me. Among them was a girl who took drugs and she wanted to beat me up because I refused to give her 30 pesos to buy crystal meth. I don't know from where the other youngsters came right then, but they surrounded me. And this did scare me. But I faced up to the kid, according to me very bravely, and I said, "Go ahead. Come on and let's see what happens."

And the only thing she said to me is, "I don't hit you because I respect your gray hair."

But since I pretended not to be afraid, I said to her, "Well don't respect my gray hair and if you want the 30 pesos come and get them." Well, now she didn't feel so tough, but rather thickheaded.

The good thing is that the men did not get involved at all. The only thing they did was to shout to the kid that she should beat me up, but nothing else. I don't know who went and told the kids who were standing on the street corner. There were about 9 of them as well. Well, a quarrel broke out between the two groups and I didn't know what to do. They only thing I did was to step aside and one of the kids from the *colonia* took me home. I was so angry and also so scared that they were going to do something to me. But everything turned out all right.

Since the *colonia* was formed there have always been fights between the gangs of *colonia*s Satélite and Unión de Residentes Lázaro Cárdenas. Unfortunately, those from the *colonia* have sometimes lost, because even deaths have resulted when the others came to their homes and to shoot them down. And they have fired off munitions on the bridge that divides the *colonias* and people have been taken to the hospital. And not one of the police has done anything to investigate. And also thee are some boys who are in jail through the fault of the other gang that implicated them in murders they seem not to have been guilty of.

I don't stick my hands in the fire even for them because in their houses some of the boys are very serious and respectful, but on the street and once on drugs they change and they have another mentally. But up until now, as I mentioned previously, I have not had any problems with them. This is my version concerning these boys from the *colonia*.

All these kind of problems have roots. As I mentioned how we as parents don't give them attention and do not know what kind of people they are hanging out with. I have noticed that contemporaneously they do not respect even their parents. I have seen 9 or 10 year old children smoking. And I do not know where they buy the cigarettes or who buys the cigarettes for them.

Chapter 7. Unión de Residentes Lazaro Cardenas III: Life in the *Colonia*

I feel sad about how the young girls who just left primary school and are beginning junior high school (*secundaría*) and they become pregnant. They have to leave their studies to go around in the street and they do not think about what will happen to themselves, burdened with an unwanted child just for not having taken care of themselves. And the worse case is that the mother, besides not having taken care of her daughter, is responsible for a grandchild fathered by an irresponsible kid. And we as mothers have the blame for not guiding our children. Even though they teach them about sex in school, they engage in it only as an experiment. It is not the same because for the youth it is just one more subject in school, but they do not put having protection in practice. The worst of all things is that they are young girls, 12 to 14 years old.

They are isolated cases, but there are these girls in the *colonia*. Their mamas, very trusting that they are going off to study, are not careful about whether they are attending school or not or simply go off to somewhere else. They never check what they are being taught and what they are given for homework. They are girls and boys that were born in the *colonia* and grew up without discipline because their mothers go to work in a maquiladora and, naturally, their fathers as well, and the children remain alone in the house.

When the *colonia* was formed, everything was different. Our children grew up in a good environment. One could walk on the streets without problems. All of us greeted one another as though we were in one big family. At Christmas we came out to give each other a hug, and the same on New Year's. At the beginning the children we brought alone with us went to swim in the canal that ran by the *colonia*. We *señoras* went into them to wash clothes. We filled the barrels for domestic water use there. We invited each other to drink coffee and the children played in the street at night with the light of bonfires or candles. In one word, we had no services. We put lime in the water we got out of the canals to rid it of the dirt, and it became very clean. It was very nice. Our children treated the elderly with respect. It was another generation. But they grew up, they married, and everything changed with their children. They didn't lack for anything, because they didn't have to suffer like their parents.

At first the children, unkempt, naked, and all burnt from the sun and the canal water until their hair was bleached—they were happy. It was the first generation to receive the certificate of completion of primary school from the school that was built in the *colonia* with the help of all of the possessors of our residential lots: a little school made of pieces of rails and ply wood. Even though not all of the children continued studying—because their parents did not have the economic means—they got work in order to help their parents out. And others continued studying until they had a career— even if it was just a technical one. And the other children are among those who became delinquents because they were not guided by their parents, or simply because they did not have sufficient care when they entered into their adolescence. And they turned toward the easiest way—drugs. They began to smoke marijuana and even to inhale crystal meth. And this is partially the cause of why their children also continue with the same, the boy kids to steal, and the girls with the circle of boys on their same level. And the other girls, as they grew up, as I mentioned previously, stopped studying because of the mistake of getting pregnant, without any notion of what a responsibility it is to be a mother.

It is easy to criticize other people without stopping to think why their children reacted this way—if they had been traumatized when little, what happened to them, or what they saw. We don't know. Then they followed the idea of doing it with other people. I am acquainted with young men who are in jail for murders they committed while stealing to get money for their drugs, or simply are complicit in these murders. And they were the same children we saw so happily playing in the streets when the *colonia* was first formed.

One of my sons wanted to break the rules in our house and go about with a group when he was 16 years old—a group that according to them went around convincing other youth to stop using drugs. They made signs and hung them up on the electricity posts and on the fences. They held concerts to earn funds to donate to the rehabilitation centers. I was worried about him, because the police could take him in for putting this type of sign on fences, even though I knew they were not printed, because at times they made them in the house. But their type of dressing, with black jackets containing lettering on them, and going about with dyed hair, gave an impression I did not like.

Because of this I was very afraid and even more when he told me, mother, we are going to have a jam session (*tocada*) in a certain place--because that is what they called the concerts that they put on. And I asked him, "Where is it going to be? Because I will be watching you."

"Ay, mother. If you want to go I will take you." The entry fee was to bring canned food or clothing in good condition.

"Fine. I want to go."

I told a very dear friend whom I trusted a lot and we went with my son and some other friends of his. We dressed in black clothing so as not to call the attention of the others--and also because it was a requisite to wear black. And we took along canned food and entered. They introduced us to their other friends. Also present were older people, also dressed in black. It looked like a convention of crows. And the music began--music that I never understood, because it was at full volume.

But when I got rid of the doubts about what they were doing, I felt more tranquil. And then my son said to me, "Mother, one day we are going to see the world in another way when we become conscious and all this corruption and badly run government is ended. And I am never going to get my voter's credential because the very government only has us as one number more on its list."

He had many sorts of strange ideas and I let him believe what he wished. I just had the idea that he would change his ideas. That it was because he was very young and didn't know what he was talking about. Well, he got married, and stayed the same. Now he even takes his little girl and his wife to his famous jam sessions. He is very responsible with his family but his ideas about changing the world do not go away.

My two eldest sons were calmer. They always went about together. They liked to go to the discotheques. They went with friends of their own age to dance to "Disco" music. My other son, among those in the middle, has been and is since a child a little more rebellious. But we have controlled him. He believes he knows everything and does not let us reprimand him. He almost wants to shut up his siblings and I. It makes us angry but we do not listen to him. Of my three daughters, each one has her own life, but they were also very obedient. I never had any problems with them when they were single.

As to the youngest of them all, I can say he has always been over-protected by his siblings since he was a child. His father was the one who scolded him most, and since he didn't allow himself to be scolded, his father insulted him. And most of all when he woke him up to take him to sell newspapers. And my son was always reading a book—I don't know where he got it from—and said to his papa, "Here it says that parents shouldn't exploit their children who are underage, and you are doing it." It seem that it was the Federal Labor Law (*Ley Federal de Trabajo*). I don't know if it said it there, but with this book he defended himself, according to him

Well his father did a half turn and said to me, "This bastard does get to me."

I have heard it said that when the offspring are still children there were not so many problems because with a slap to the rump if they engaged in some mischief they remained subdued, but when they grew up you couldn't hit them anymore. Well, I have indeed given them slaps if they said a curse word in front of me. If they have a good foundation in the home, there is no age that they cannot be reprimanded.

I have not been a perfect mother either, but seeing how the environment in this *colonia* has changed, I recommend to my grandchildren that they be careful. that they don't get mixed up in anything bad, and that when they visit me, they pay attention to who comes near them and with what intentions. Even though the majority of people know me, an unknown person could come around and you don't know whom they are. Because there are those children who walk along with their heads bowed, and their cell phones in their hands, and they don't pay attention to who is near them.

And a boy from the *colonia* stole a cell phone from my oldest grandson. And they robbed a bicycle from my next oldest grandson. Because my grandchildren were confident that everyone is the same. They stole from the only store in the *colonia*, and the cell phone was on the curb in front of the house. And two boys passed by and they took it and ran. And the good thing is that my grandson was able to recognize them: that they were from the *colonia*, and knew where they get together. And he showed me who they were. So I went to protest, but they did not want to give it to me. Then I went to talk to one of their mothers, but she said she didn't know what her children were up to. Since she went to work, she was aware of nothing. And she didn't know where the other boy was from. I believe he was from the *colonia* on the other side of the highway (Rivera Campestre).

There are kids who don't even want to go to school and spend their time stealing in order to buy drugs. And one must be careful with these boys. One knows them by sight, but one doesn't know what intentions they have. They are between 16 and 18 years old.

That is, then, the community where we are living. Now it is not like when the majority of us could sleep in the yard, protecting ourselves from mosquitos with smoke from a fire. Or at times we had to make canopies with mosquito netting. We could leave our clothes hanging out and no one would steal them. Nothing happened on our grounds and we did not even have fences, but all was good. And now you cannot even leave a broom out, because it will disappear. Almost all of us have fences around our houses, but even so the thieves jump over them and take what they can.

The thieves have left *señoras* without blankets when the *señoras* wash them and hang them out to dry during the night. In the morning they go to take them in, and what a surprise, they find nothing there. And the worst of all is the thieves go around selling them nearby where they robbed them. Once it happened to me, but with some chairs I rented out to a family that was having a party. [Ernestina and her son Guillermo make some money renting out chairs and tables for parties.] And when we went to get them, two were missing. And the *señora* of the house, very pained, said, "Ernestina, if they don't turn up somewhere because some neighbor took them, I will have to pay you for them."

"Good. I will wait awhile, and if you don't find them, well, I am sorry."

And so two weeks went by and there was no news about the chairs. But a boy appeared with two chairs wanting to sell them to me, since he knew I had chairs to rent out. And he offered them to me at 50 pesos each one. And I told him that, yes, I would buy them. I took them, put them inside the house, while he waited outside on the curb for the money. And I came out and told him thanks, but without the money. And he said to me, you haven't given me the cash for the chairs. And I said to him, "Look, go inside and look at what it says below the seats." And there was written "Ibarbol." Well they had stolen these chairs from the *señora* who rented them from me. "And thank you for bringing them to me, because I am not going to give you anything."

Well, the boy left, probably saying to himself, how come I didn't notice that they were labeled? I went to the *señora* to tell her that she not be worried--that I had gotten the chairs back. Well, very content, she thanked me.

A similar thing happened to a neighbor of mine. Two blankets disappeared from the clothesline where she had them drying. And the next day the robbers went to sell them to her. And she got them back too. And the worst thing about it was that it was the son of one of her *comadres*.

The worst of all are young men who have grown up in the same community but were out of control of their parents and were victims of anyone who entrapped them and little by little became accustomed to using drugs, and if they did not work, well they dedicated themselves to stealing from anyone who let them of who they caught off guard.

They have not taken anything from me personally. To the contrary they come around and offer to throw out the garbage or bring firewood they collected to sell me, and I buy it from them. And I give something to those who take away the garbage that I have in garbage bags, and I do it in order to gain their trust in case one day I find myself in the street with some problem, so I will have someone to defend me. Because they are not stupid--they know who treats them badly, and who does not. Or simply if something happens to one of my children they come by and tell me. Up to know nothing has presented itself, and I hope it doesn't. But equally, if one of them has a problem, why can't I help him? Thus one gains their trust. The *colonia* is not so big that we can be enemies.

There are also several families who got their immigration papers as *Rodinos* [under the 1986 Immigration Reform and Control Act, sponsored by Senator Rodino] and go to work in the United States in order to give their offspring a better standard of living and so they will continue studying and have a university career and better their lives.

Other married couples did not have the economic resources to give a basic education to their children. But they have taught them to respect others and they taught them to work and not to fall into the web of drug or alcohol abuse.

Now it is no longer like when the *colonia* began to take form. If there was a party at any house, we attended even if we were not invited. They took care of us as though we were. It was joyful. The invited us to dine and to dance until the dance was over, and nothing happened. And if the following week there was another party we all got together again and the same thing happened. But now you don't even hear music. If there is some party, perhaps a birthday party for someone in the family, only those who are invited are welcome. And since almost everyone has fenced in ptheir houses, there is no way to get in. And maybe also they do it for security, that no one comes to disrupt the ambiance.

When it was joyful at the parties, those who came to disrupt the ambiance were two brothers that all of us knew. But they didn't come to start a fight. They came drunk, almost falling down, and asked women to dance. They didn't care if the women were with their husbands or boyfriends. And if the women refused to dance with them, they pulled them out to the dance area by force. But we sent to ask their mother to take them home, and she dragged them by their ears and took them home to sleep. And the ambiance continued. And the hostess of the party said to the *señora* that after she got her sons to bed, she should return to dance awhile.

The mother of these boys was a very nice *señora*, and very respected by us, very humble, but with a good heart. But her sons were little drunks that made her angry, and that is when they had to face the music. Poor *señora*, that was her cross, her sons and her husband, the three of them going around drunk together. Finally she fled to another colonia to live with her daughters. They were married by then and had started their own families, but the sons stayed in the *colonia*. But now they are alcoholics, and nobody listens to them.

At that time I was the *colonia*'s representative and there were no lack of people that invited me to be a godmother for a fifteen year old (*quinceañera*). There were at least seven, and I was also a godmother for a wedding. Since the people knew I loved to party, there I was. Everything was organized at home. Nothing involved a salon. All of the godmothers were from the same community. It was easier for them to come to a party in the *colonia* and besides renting a salon was very dear. What we paid for was the music. And we also went to ask the municipal police to send us a patrol car in case someone caused a rumble. So we had to pay a fee to the police commissioner, so that there would not be any fights caused by some impertinent drunk.

All these memories come into my mind as though I were living them, but they are only memories, if very happy in terms of our lives together. Some bad memories also come to my mind. Like when we had to guard the entrances to the *colonia*. When the *señores* had to be on guard to make sure more people did not enter to invade lots, because not all lots were inhabited at the time, or simply so that the police did not enter to remove us.

There were two very aggressive *señores* who always carried machetes in their belts. And we had each one of them guarding the two entrance ways. But the other *señores* did not know the extent of their aggressiveness. They took up their machetes for whatever circumstance they did not like. One was from Durango and the other from Nayarit. Well, the one from Durango was called Terso and had a wife and two little girls. And the one from Nayarit was also married and had one son and two daughters. He was named Isidro. I don't remember the names of their wives. The wives almost never left their houses, not even when we had a neighborhood meeting.

Well Isidro wounded a comrade who was on guard with him with his machete and they had to take him to the Red Cross. Isidro cut him on his arm. Isidro did not stay long in the colonia. People didn't want to have him there because he often beat his wife and his children. Later we learned that he had been killed. And the other "cane-cutter" (*machetero*)—that is what we nicknamed them—also had to leave, and also because his neighbors were terrorized. He wanted to cut us with his machete.

This cane-cutter, Terso, lived nearby us. And one day we were talking to one of his neighbors and the neighbor complained to us that every now and then Terso came to bother his wife and also others who lived nearby. Every once in awhile he insulted them and threatened them with the machete. That he--the neighbor--was afraid to leave his family alone because the cane-cutter might do something to them. And we were talking about this when the cane-cutter appeared and entered our lot with a machete in his hand.

I was very frightened that he was going to hit the *señor* and my son who drove the water truck, with his machete. And we didn't know what to do. He claimed he was coming to kill the *señor* who had come to complain to us. And he started swinging the machete in all directions. But one of the times he swung the machete it slipped out of his hands and landed beneath the water truck. And at that point the neighbor grabbed the cane-cutter and threw him on the ground and hit him. And then my husband went to call for the police, and they handcuffed him and took him away. And they had to go to lodge a complaint so they would pass him on to the court. He was very beaten up and they took the machete as evidence. Since then we know nothing about him.

His wife left the house with their daughters. I believe, it seems, they went back to where they had come from. She also was from Durango. And we never again saw the famous cane-cutter. But the man who had been cut by the machete while on guard continued to live in the colonia for a while. Then he went and sold his house. As was the case with other families, we never saw him again.

That was another chapter about our little colonia, that is at times conflict-ridden. Now the main street is paved and we do not know what kind of people transit it. Now one is concerned about sending the children alone to the store. It is preferable to send someone older or go ourselves. By 7 at night it is very dangerous for a child to walk the streets alone. At times the children play on our street but we must be careful: there are people watching them and they also take care of one another.

My grandchildren also come by and start playing in the street in front of the house. I just tell them to take care, and to let us know if they see anyone suspicious passing by. But those who pass by are the very boys I know, who are addicted to drugs. But they don't do anything. They go their own way. There are times they stop to watch the children playing, and then they move on.

Among these boys I am referring to are the sons of a married couple that is now deceased, and they remain alone in the house even though they have many more siblings. But no one aided them in time, and they became drug addicts. They always go about gathering up whatever materials are thrown out so they can sell them to keep up their addiction and to eat. When they come to my house asking me to sell them some cooked beans, they now know that I will give the beans to them whenever I have some. If I make flour tortillas I give them to the boys to eat with their beans and if I make salsa I give them a little bag of it, and they go away content. When I collect plastic bottles and put them into a bag, I give them to the boys, or also some electrical appliance that no longer works. And they take the electrical goods away and take out the copper and sell it.

It is one way to have them on my side if something happens. I know whom I can count on. They are honorable boys, but unfortunately, their vices have overtaken them, and their siblings do not give them any attention. Well, the way they are, I believe it is too late. It is a family of more than 20 siblings and they could do something for these boys, who are not really boys anymore. They are adults.

I don't judge anyone, because everyone has his or her own vices. But I wish with all my heart that someone would give them guidance and that they would rid them of these so deeply rooted addictions that are destroying them.

Chapter 8. Other Invasions

Invasion of Nueva Alameda

There was another invasion in which I participated at the invitation of some leaders from other *colonias* who asked me to support them. But I had another interest as well: that they grant a lot to my eldest son, Antonio. And on this condition I felt encouraged to take part. But my pleasure lasted for just a little while because these lands were the property of SARH—*Secretaría de Agricultura y Recursos Hidráulicos* (Secretariat of Agriculture and Hydraulic Resources)—destined to house their employees. The settlement lasted for a while, I don't remember how long, about two months. But in these two months we had to stand guard at each entrance to the invasion.

We were approximately 300 or 400 families and on each street we were responsible to guard against the arrival of the state police, because a lawsuit had been leveled on those leaders who were to blame. And since we knew who was responsible for the invasion, we had to defend the cause, even with the clubs that they gave us in case we saw anyone suspicious and for when we stood guard at night. If someone unknown entered they alerted us with firecrackers like those they use in the fireworks at town fairs. And it was exciting for me to take part in the invasion, because I was not participating as a leader, but indeed as an invader like the other comrades.

And it fell to me to be a guard on my street and with luck nothing happened. But when I was sleeping in my little room made of tarpaulins, a firecracker was fired off to alert the comrades not to let anyone enter the invasion. And thus it was daily. There were times it fell to me to be on guard duty from 10 p.m. to 6 a.m. together with other comrades, building bonfires and drinking coffee that other comrades cooperated to bring us.

And it also fell to my son to stand guard duty. Everything went well until the police came for one of the leaders and took him away. But there was a protest movement [described below] and they let him go. But we had to negotiate with the governor who sent a delegate to dialogue with us and with the other leaders. And that is when they moved us to another *colonia*, called "Solidaridad."

Well, it occurred to the delegate to come once again to Nueva Alameda, and we made a human circle surrounding him and we did not let him go. The famous delegate was Rafael Morgan from the PAN party (*Partido Acción Nacional*, National Action Party, a business oriented political party) and we told him that not until we saw our leader arrive free again would we let him go. The leader was Javier Saldivie, nicknamed "Pitufo." And so it was that they sent for him to be released from jail so we would let the delegate go.

The police also arrived—we were surrounded by police—but it didn't matter to us. They released Pitufo, we let the delegate go, and the police relocated us to empty lots in Solidaridad. They also gave my son a lot. Antonio was building his little room when a leader (female) arrived and asked him to pass on the lot to a girl who was a single mother, and as soon as they found another lot they would give it to him. And my good-natured son told her yes. But it turned out that this single mother had been a neighbor and a friend of my offspring in the colonia where we lived previously, Miraflores, as already mentioned. Well my son had to leave her the lot with the little room he was building. He felt sorry for her children and now didn't want to know anything more about the famous house lots. I don't even know if she still lives there.

In the end, the lot that the leader (female) had promised Antonio was never turned over. We did not want to be insistent and we retired from this invasion. Antonio went to Rosarito, married there, and bought a little land, and built on it for the family. I dedicated myself to helping Adolfo with the sales of oil and lubricants for cars at our stall on the side of they highway, and to my domestic duties, and to send my children to school, some to primary school, some to secondary and preparatory school. It was very debilitating work for me, but it was my responsibility as a mother. I didn't want my children to be dirty or go without eating, because they also worked helping their papa to sell newspapers, and they came home tired and in a hurry to bathe themselves and go to school. And I wanted them to go with their stomachs full even if they had to eat rapidly to go on time. But I was satisfied with my responsibilities, and had time for everything.

Invasion of San Juan de las Pulgas

Later, another leader, from an *ejido* in the Mexicali Valley, asked me to invite people from my *colonia* to go to support an invasion of some lands beside the ocean, near Ensenada. These lands had owners. They were a group of *ejitatarios* from the agrarian organization we belonged to, and they wanted us to come. We were only three families because others were afraid that harm could befall them. But other families from the Valley went. Well, in the beginning we gathered together about 30 people. But we were not successful because drug traffickers were monopolizing these lands. They had their center of operations there, and we had little power. During the night they began shooting off bullets and to tell the truth, I was scared. But we stayed there, with our fear, for two months.

And I said to my husband that I didn't want to be there because it was very dangerous even though our comrades stood guard. Even so we were all in danger. Once when I went to leave groceries for my papa and myself, I told him, "I want to go back to Mexicali! I don't want to stay! What if they decide to come and kill us one night? I want to leave!" Because when we were invited, no one told us that these drug traffickers were living there.

My husband said, "If you want to go, gather together what we brought and we will stop by to leave your papa in Rosarito." But my papa didn't want to leave. He said, "I am staying. If they kill us, well we die in the struggle. I won't give up. After all, now I am here."

Then I advised the other families that had come with me from Mexicali that I was leaving. I asked if they wanted to stay or if the would leave with us. And one of the families said to me, "We too are going, because it is oppressive to put oneself in danger with these people"—referring to the drug traffickers. So, we left. I no longer wanted to know anything about this invasion.

Well, since my papa was always very friendly, he became friends with those who were guarding the cargo of drugs. He became close to them. But he didn't count on the fact that one night the drug traffickers would begin to burn down the little rooms that had been built by the invaders. The leader of the organization to which we belonged had taken everyone to a meeting in Ensenada and when they returned at night they found that all was burned down and that they had to leave the place. And they burned down the little room belonging to my papa made of new wooden boards that Adolfo had bought for him. And they stole all the plates and cookware I had given him and everything else that we had left. The only thing that he could save was a big pot made of thick aluminum where a friend of mine from the group and I made coffee for everyone. But they, stubborn, had wanted to stay.

From the time I arrived at that place I commented that those people made me suspicious. But I was told that they were trustworthy and were those who were taking care that no one entered. Because other people had gone there wishing to invade, and were not allowed, but we were going to be allowed to. And what was our surprise when they didn't open the fence for us—because everything was closed in with barbed wire. So we had to pull down the fence in order to get in. And of course this bothered them, even though they said nothing to us. But I guess that they mentioned it to the boss and that is why what happened later—they destroyed everything of ours. But we were all right in the beginning. And by then we had planned where we were going to build the school, put the residential lots and the playground for the children, and everything else. Everything had been planned out.

Well, I liked this place very much because we were about 500 meters from the ocean, even though there was no beach. But there were cliffs and we could climb down them to pick up shellfish and squid. For the two months I was there I was very content. The problem was that we had entered the mouth of the dragon. I have nothing else to say beyond these commentaries, because I withdrew in time.

As far as the other families go I found out later from my papa that they moved to Maneadero, a locality near Ensenada, B.C. It seems they went to ask for housing lots, and were given them. The families I took along returned to Mexicali. They too did not want to have anything more to do with the invasion. My papa returned to his normal life in Rosarito.

I call it an invasion because we went to invade a piece of land that did not belong to us, although it supposedly belonged to some *ejidatarios* who wanted to get it back. But we hadn't known that drug traffickers had occupied it, and the *ejidatarios* pushed us forward into the storm. But we couldn't do anything about the drug traffickers. All these *ejidatarios* had their residential center near the invasion. And it was called Ejido Eréndira. It is a locality that was established many years ago, though I am not sure how many. But the people have all the services (electricity, running water, etc.). The locality belongs to the delegation of Santo Tomás, municipality of Ensenada. (p. 167).

According to my papa's version, it seems that they captured the boss of this mafia and returned the lands to their legitimate owners. Those who had been taking care of the lands had to withdraw from them. And that is all I know about this famous invasion.

During this time I was not aware of the consequences and problems I got involved in. I liked the excitement. But as the years pass it is no longer the same. One becomes more cowardly about confronting everything. Previously, it wasn't important to me if they arrested me and took me to jail—that just gave me strength to continue fighting for the common good.

And now, also, invasions are prohibited and I am not going to put myself at risk. Now I do not have the same energy to go about as an invader, acquiring land for other people. Now let everyone scratch with their own fingernails. In its time I helped them a lot, as much as I could, without receiving any economic advantage. I never liked corruption. I always did it with my own means. I wasn't rich but I at least had enough to pay bus fare with the help of my work—selling newspapers.

I narrate all this because I like to remember the experiences I passed through. Of course, no one forced me to do it! As I said previously, I enjoyed it. Now I had my plot of land to live on. It would have cost me nothing to be peaceful, but I wanted to participate in helping families who had no patrimony for their offspring, although I never took advantage: I own just my little piece of land where I have my house. It wouldn't have cost me anything to have taken over more land, like the other leaders do: in every invasion they obtained lots even though they didn't occupy them, and later on they passed them on to other families in exchange for money. That was their way of helping.

Well, I believe that it was a lovely epoch for me. It's a shame I don't have the same strength! I worked as hard as I could. Now I have a pension, from working in the trucking warehouse. Social Security doesn't give me much but I receive something for all my efforts made during the years I worked. Almost all my children are married. Only my youngest son remains at home. I hope he will marry some day. I don't know what he will decide because nothing cooks at the first boiling (*no se cuece al primer hervor*—you can lead a horse to water but you can't make him drink), as we say.

For me it was very exciting to have had the opportunity to help or support families so that the would have a little piece of land to live on, even if it was through invasions. Because even I have the little piece of land where I am living currently though this means. And it was convenient for the government to accept these invasions, because through them they earned economically by charging for the land and services in installments, not very high ones, but they did charge us. But the same government was in agreement to pay the owners of the invaded lands though the State Real Estate Office—in case the lands had owners.

But there were also invasions of federal lands, such as on the edges of highways, canals, and rivers. And while the government was not using these zones, people stayed there to live, until they were run off. But if the government didn't run them off, the people would begin to build houses of solid materials. The only problem is that they will never have land titles, nor are they paying for services because they do not receive these benefits.

Today, contemporaneously, what the government has opted to do is to make agreements with building companies to construct social housing and sell it through INFONAVIT for the employees of maquiladoras and charge them though their payroll taxes within a lapse of 30 years, and with low installments. And today, as well, whomever organizes a land invasion is punished by being jailed.

Now what the state government is doing is to pass all residential lots that are not inhabited to the municipality so it will put these lots up for auction and thus recuperate the money owed for property taxes. And he who desires to and has the money can buy one of these lots. This seems a perfect plan to me—because these people are keeping us from having the most necessary services, and because they never inhabited their lots or paid property taxes.

Well, right now in my *colonia* we have the three basic services: running water, electricity, and sewerage. We are lacking pavement on the streets but what is causing most harm is that the very people of the community are throwing their garbage in a canal that once served to irrigate the fields that surround us on two sides. The Secretariat of Agriculture and Hydraulic Resources (SARH) cut off the water to the canal because it was no longer necessary. No one was growing anything in the neighboring fields. Now it is being exploited as a garbage dump and the municipality hasn't done anything about putting up a sign prohibiting the dumping of garbage. And all this is a focus of infection, because they even throw dead animals into it, and no one is capable of saying anything.

At times I do not like to be so detailed about everything that has happened to me, but if I do not relate it in this way, I feel that it is nothing more than a narrative, and thus it would have no meaning to tell about part of my life and what has happened to me in the family nucleus. Of course I do not remember everything, because I would have to have an excellent memory. But there are things I do remember about the father of my children, while we were together, like his being attentive to my children when they were in school. He was the one who went to the parents' meetings. And when he came back from work he went to ask the teachers how the children were doing with their grades, and how they behaved in class. He also went to collect them and brought them home along with some little neighbors who lived on the same street.

But at times my children didn't like it, and they said, "Mama, we don't want my father to go to the assembly hall, because he is very loud-mouthed and we are embarrassed that he is like than. And if we are at recess he shouts for us, looking for us until he finds us." But this seemed all right to me, because almost no other father went to ask about their children. Even if he was loud-mouthed, the good thing was that they knew he was.

And the teachers held up my children as an example to other students. And they told them, "It would be good if your father worried about you a little as does the father of the García Ibarbol's, and that you learn from them. Even though the whole family works, they always bring in their homework and never miss classes. And I have problems about getting the homework from you even if you don't work."

There were times when the father of my children exaggerated his strictness with them. Adolfo wanted them to do nothing but study and that they tell him everything they had learned, and if they didn't, he did not let them out to play. And he said to my children that they had nothing to do on the street, they were not worthy of going even out to the sidewalk, and he wanted the to do nothing more than study. I couldn't say anything to him because he immediately shut me up. I truly do not know how he let me become the representative of the *colonia* [U.R.L.C.] and permitted me to take official documents in to the government agencies and go about with leaders from other *colonias*.

But at times he was good, when he finished working on week ends and took them to the movies, or simply took them for a day out, or took them for Chinese food. I remained behind to do the housework. But when he suddenly got enraged, all of us hid. I believe even the dog was afraid of him.

I remember one time that he arrived from work very angry and I didn't know what had happened to him. Perhaps it was a gal who rejected him, because indeed he was very much a womanizer. He believed that I did not know it, but it was easy to see. Well that day he arrived and even kicked the dog, and he arrived like an ogre, using many swear words. And we were better off paying no attention to him. And little by little he calmed down. After awhile he was talking nicely to us. I didn't want to ask him anything. The only thing I did was to tell him to come to eat, and he ate well, as though nothing had happened.

This situation with him made me think he was bipolar. I was just waiting to see how he came home, content or angry. It could also be that he drank continuously—he changed when he didn't have a drop of alcohol in his head. But he also drank beer to the point of falling down and began insulting anyone who was around. I didn't know how to handle him. He was very insulting and somewhat of a despot.

Well, I went along bearing it for 25 years. The only thing I liked—I am not going to deny it—is how he took care of his children. For the time he was with us, my children never went hungry. He brought cans of tuna fish to my oldest two daughters because they liked it a lot. And he said, "I brought each of my daughters a can of tuna fish so that they don't get angry that I brought it for only one." And the others ate whatever he brought, they did not lack for beans, potatoes, eggs, and tortillas and, yes, many vegetables. And since he liked making salads, he had them eat what he made.

As concerns this, I have nothing to say. And he said to me, "Make them something to take along so that they don't go around hungry, or I will give them money there, at school." But they didn't need money because they had some coins that they had been given as tips for the newspaper sales. It is true I never sent them to school in dirty or un-ironed uniforms. They were always very tidy. All those things that happened to my children at their father's side were things that because of their young age they did not realize what their father was like. And they wanted to have a childhood, like others.

And when Adolfo left us, they were grown up. The youngest in the family was 14 years old. And I thank him for having taught them to work, and to have been careful that nothing happened to them, and also that they didn't go around with kids who had neither a career nor a benefit (*ni oficio ni beneficio*--neither a present nor a future).

He left exactly when we reached twenty-five years of marriage. He fled with a woman from our *colonia*. And he left with her twenty-one years ago. On the one hand it is good that he distanced himself from us. That way we were not waiting to see if he came home angry or content. The only thing I am sorry for is that she left her children with her husband. She came back for them ten years later, but with deceptions, saying they were going on vacation to the D.F. Meanwhile, she and Adolfo had relocated to Mexico City.

But back then they had evolved a plan, because she left two months earlier, and then he went. And when we found out, they were already together, and she put the three children in a boarding school, so that they would not bother her and Adolfo. But their father, my *compadre*, realized how they were living and he went to fetch the two eldest, and he brought them up.

On our side, we continued on with our lives. My sister-in-law --Adolfo's sister--took my youngest, Memo, to study in secondary school in the D.F. He was there for 3 years. Shortly before the adulterers left he saw all their debauchery. And my two eldest daughters went to study at a teachers' training school in Chihuahua, but prior to the time their father left. All this debauchery occurred after my children had grown up. Their father was old enough to know better and think about the fact that he was no longer a young man to go about being a womanizer.

Perhaps there were more bad things, but I have to recognize that not everything is rose-colored. I would have liked to have a lovely marriage such as I dreamed about when I was single.

When Adolfo left, he left us in a little house roofed with plastic sheets and with walls covered by cardboard.. Fortunately we had some rooms made of solid material—bricks—when he left and abandoned us, and we built that which was lacking.

At this time I began to work in a housing development that had just been completed. I went and asked for work, and they gave it to me. It consisted of removing all the debris that the construction workers had left inside the houses. And with what they paid me, I went along buying a little cement, sand, and wood, so as to finish up the house.

I mention all this because we did suffer for a while, until we found ourselves and organized ourselves to move forward. I told my children, "We have suffered greater injuries and all this is minimal for me. So, my children, we must move forward. We are not going to cry just because your father has abandoned us." Of course he offended us in the beginning, but afterwards we didn't even remember it. And until today the only thing we have said is to accept it for its good side.

Ten years later he came back to look for his children as though nothing had happened. And I never tried to stop them from seeing him. He is their father and if they want to see him, then that is their problem. The only thing I said to them was, "Don't think about letting him inside the house because you will see what I am capable of. I will call the police so they take him away." Because he swore to me once in a while that he would never return the day he left the house. He threatened me with that every once in awhile, as if I were going to weep and beg him not to leave me. He threatened me with this every day until he finally left. But as they saying goes, there is no bad thing from which a good thing doesn't arise (*no hay mal que por bien no venga*).

He believed that once he left, none of my children would come to see me, and he was completely wrong. We remained together and they helped one another out.

When anyone had a problem they helped one another mutually. If one of them did not have money at the moment, he asked for a loan from one of his sisters, even if it was not going to be repaid. But they loaned money among themselves and if they lacked money later on, they did the same. And they said, "Now you owe me such and such and I have a little savings account with you," and they started to laugh.

Perhaps there are women among us who far from inculcating respect for their father, speak ill of him in front of his children. And if they want to listen to this they are going to do so, and yes, about all the bad that a suffering mother has experienced beside her husband. That is a problem between them and the children should not be involved. And in the end, if the children want to be beside their papa, they will be. And it is best that they alone make the decision. I myself never told them not to talk to him. The only thing I said to them was to do what their consciences dictated. If they wanted to receive him, then receive him. Now they are older. But this too, has led to nothing. I said, "Or if one of you comes with him and lets him in, for him the doors are closed since a long time ago." And as they saying goes, he who leaves his home, leaves his cup (*él que va de su casa pierde su tasa*), and now he has lost it.

I have always told them that I am not angry that he left, it took a cactus spine from on top of me. But I do have feelings about it, because he made me the unhappiest woman on the earth by the way he left. Because he left with a person that not only did I esteem so very much that we almost ate from the same plate, but she also was godmother to almost everyone in the family. [She was Ernestina and Adolfo's *comadre*]. She never left my house. She, together with her children, almost slept in my house. And to pay me back with this deceit! I trusted this woman very much. Even my friends withdrew from me because of this woman. I could not believe it the day I found out she was going around with my husband. The world caved in on me. And with reason her mother-in-law fought with her every once in awhile. And I was defending her.

And my husband was chasing my friends away. Most probably he believed they were going to gossip to me about what they saw. Well, he was not so wrong. They came and told me they had seen him with this woman. And I didn't completely believe them because she always visited me at the same time every day. But I didn't know this man (Adolfo) waited for me to fall asleep, and then left in the night. Or simply he did not sleep in the same room as I did, so he could leave at night and then return. When I got up he was in his bed, and the devil came back early so that I would not suspect anything.

And then she came with her little mosquito face and said it looked like her *compadre* (Adolfo) had another woman. That she had seen her. And she even described the aforementioned. And she insisted that if I wished she herself would take me to where this woman lived. And I, like a fool, accepted her game. The two of us went off to protest to this woman.

When I refer to and say that woman (her *comadre*) it is because at times I do not wish to even mention her name—I was so tremendously angry. That this anger I believe converted to fury with the desire to confront her and beat her into pieces, not to eat them, because she would be dead, and also because of the poison in her body. Not even to the dogs would I feed her meat: what guilt have the dogs? Rather to throw the pieces into the garbage--because that which she did to me is not worthy of a friend.

159

And I so naïve that I accompanied her to complain to the woman that she said was going around with my husband.

But what happened is that I got angry and directed my attention to the other woman [who lives in Solidaridad. She was Ernestina's neighbor in Nueva Alameda, the invasion from which the invaders were transferred to lots in Solidaridad]. And she still wanted me to beat her up, but I didn't wish to accompany her. Later I went alone, and yes, it was true. She confessed it to me. But she told me that it was long ago since she had anything to do with him. And Adolfo even had a son with her.

I did not get angry. The only thing I told her was to take very good care of her boy and that if my husband wanted to visit the child I would permit it, so that he knew whom his father was.

The good thing was that she was a single mother and had a son apart from Adolfo's baby. When I went to talk to the girl (Teresa) the baby was a year and six months old and it was not until then that I knew about this relation. I never accepted it, but as they say, out of sight, out of mind (*ojos que no ven, corazón que no siente*). And my children went to become acquainted with their half-brother, and I did not oppose it, because there have been so many cases that without learning or knowing people enter into amorous relationships among themselves. Nor did they let me know when they went to see this child, believing I would get angry.

And much later I found out from one of my sons that his mother worked in the same maquiladora as he did. He told me what they spoke of together, and he said to me, "Mama, I have no reason not to talk to this woman, because I have to handle things at work. I am line supervisor and we get along very well. And she told me about my half-brother. She said he was studying in the university and that she was going to go to work in the United States, and now had a *señor* whom she was going to marry. And she

160

was going to leave the house my father built for her to her children so they could live there. I have not seen her recently. Maybe she went. The truth is, mama, I have no anger, because she built up hopes and you know my father can draw someone out until they fall in his web. And the poor girl fell like the others, even though she came from some town in the State of Mexico [where people are supposed to be more sophisticated, given that part of Mexico City encompasses a small section of that state].

"I already knew about the relationship, but I never wished to tell you, in order not to worry you. I believe that even Memito knew because when my father went to collect us from selling newspapers he took us to this house, and she came outside to receive us. And she even made us food. But it was well known that when we arrived he would send us to buy sodas, and they remained alone together. And they used "*tú*" [a familiar form of "you" used then, and still among the working class, only for very good friends and intimates]. Then when we were selling the motor oils, she came by to visit him and asked him for money, and he gave it to her. And once in awhile I saw her riding in the car with my papa, carrying wood, and after awhile he returned as though nothing had happened."

"Gustavito, I also saw her about two times, but I never imagined he was taking her to that house. And after I had seen him he arrived, and without my asking any explanation he said that the wood was for a friend (male) who was constructing a locale to sell tires, and asked him favors. I remained silent because in reality I didn't know if it was true about his other old lady (*vieja*).

She (her *comadre*) made a fool of me, saying I go to protest to her (the woman in Solidaridad), so that I would not suspect about her and Adolfo. Until I set a trap, and that is when I became disillusioned about everything. Because before I discovered them, she said she was going on vacation to Mexico City and would pass by my daughter Magali's house in Chihuahua. That she already had the address that I had given her. But since I discovered everything about them, she did not go. She went directly to Mexico City.

All these things happened after I stopped selling newspapers, because, according to my husband, it was not necessary for me to go, because I could be taking care of my children and helping them sell the motor oils-- he had put an open air stall to sell motor oils on the edge of the highway across from the entry to the *colonia* where we live. He formed a team of the children for the newspaper sales. And with the story that I had to take care of the car oils and lubricants, it happened I did not realize what was occurring. He would come to the stall and I would go home to make lunch and send my children to school.

And the old lady with whom he left spent time with him at the stall. But I never suspected anything. One thing I did notice, that was very notable, was when she arrived he got up from where he was sitting and gave her a soda, very nicely—because we also sold sodas and ice during the summer. But he never ever said to me, when you want a soda you can take one. And this remained engraved in my memory. And when we fought for whatever motive, I complained, and he said, you don't take a soda because you don't want one. And since he counted them, I was incapable of taking one. Because when he came from selling newspapers he went and counted them all and I had to give him all the money for what I'd sold, and I was afraid he would say something to me if one was missing.

What I was unable to comprehend is what he did with so much money, that he earned not only in the sale of newspapers but also in the sale of motor oils. Because it went well with him, but according to him he never had money. But he did indeed share it with the women because they wouldn't follow him around just for his pretty face.

One because of her child, the other I guess because she sold new clothing. Well, he must have given her the money to do this.

The economic situation began to get worse. I stopped wanting to help him with the motor oils and I went to work at the IFE (*Instituto Federal de Electores*, Federal Institute of Voters) as a house-to-house canvasser when they began giving out the first identifications, then without a photograph. I am talking about between 1991 and 1992. And I without having finished high school—even though high school completion was one of the requisites for being employed in this work. But since I was acquainted with the entire area I was assigned, they accepted me with my certificate of completion of primary school. They just asked that I know how to read and write, that I knew my numbers, and that I was good at spelling. I filled all of these requirements in the IFE office and immediately began to work.

Well, to make a long story short, I began earning my own money, paid every two weeks. And so my situation changed. But since my husband knew I saved a part of the money, he would arrive and shamelessly say, "You have money. Lend me 800 *pesos* and in the evening when I get the money from the newspapers or from the motor oils, I will pay you." And I, like a fool, let go of the *800* pesos—with the hope that he would return them to me.

And the evening passed by. Another day passed, another week passed, and I still waiting for the money. Until I became brave and said to him, "Pay me the money that you owe me."

And he answered, "What money? I don't owe you anything."

"And the money I lent you?"

"I don't owe you anything, and don't be screwing around with me."

Well, the money was never returned. And time passed, maybe two or three months, and he asked for a loan again, because the suppliers of the motor oil were here and he didn't have enough to pay them what he owed. "Come along now, lend me some. I know you have some saved. What does it cost you? Lend me 600 *pesos* and I will pay you back along with the other money I owe you."

And I, once again hopeful that he was going to pay me back everything, lent him money again, but advising him that he owed me a lot. "Let's see how you do it, but you are going to pay it all back."

"Of course I am going to pay you."

He never paid this money back, but I was so believing he would. Well, I gave it up for lost. And I never knew what he wanted it for, if he really was going to pay the suppliers of the motor oil or if he was going to give it to the women who asked him for money. I never investigated.

Because of this, when he left with the so-and-so, on the one hand I felt free, but on the other hand, he left me in debt with the suppliers. And time had to pass, almost eight months, before I could pay them all that was owed. As we went along selling, we paid them in installments. My son Gustavo and I kept the stall and assumed the debt. Until my son said to me, "Mama, now we have to take down the stall, so that I can concentrate on finding work and doing something to the house. Because look at the conditions my *jefe* [chief, father of the house] left us. Far from helping us he left us some ugly, dilapidated rooms. When it rains everything gets wet, since the roof is of tarpaulin."

"My son, you speak well--because I can't be running the business by myself. Better that I also find work and thus we will get ahead. Because, you see, only you and

I remain, Memito studying in Mexico City, and Marcelo in the army. There is no other choice but to work."

I didn't want to be a responsibility for my children. In the beginning it was very hard for me, the fact that the father of my children had left us. But out of every bad thing comes a good thing (*no hay mal que por bien no venga*).

When I began to look for work, I found it quickly and began to make friends with the women who worked in maintenance in a housing development. This work was very hard because one had to get rid of the rubble that the construction workers left in the apartments and houses, and the lumps of hardened cement that they left on the floors. They gave us some metal rods similar to spatulas. Even sparks flew when one could not remove the cement because it had hardened so much. And clean the windows so that no cement remained glued to them.

And since I wasn't such a dummy, I began to find a way to make it less difficult. When I entered in the morning I threw a bucket of water where the cement lumps were and I left them soaking while I cleaned the windows. And they soaked through. When I wanted to remove the cement, it detached quite easily. And the other workers began watching what I did. They said to me, "How smart you are! How is it that it didn't occur to us to do it that way, and thus finish the job earlier?" And I was making friends among the *señoras* and the girls.

There were also plumbers, electricians, and masons. Well, we got together every Saturday, since work was over at midday. There never lacked someone to buy us big bottles of beer. We got together in the house that served as a warehouse, and we put ourselves to drinking beer, with the pretext that the day was hot. And since the engineer for whom we were working also appeared, well we felt more confident. And our leader (female) began to trust me more. And she went and left me in charge. And she showed up two or three hours late and I didn't say anything to her. As long as they were paying me, it wasn't my problem.

But one day the engineer discovered her when she was arriving and he asked her if she did this every day. And no one was missing in saying yes, that she left us alone to do the work. Then she responded and said that she had left me in charge. Immediately the engineer said to her—she was a young woman—"You come with me and I am going to give you your severance pay. And give the keys to the *señora*. She is going to be in charge of the women workers and the other personnel. And if anything is needed, ask her for the materials. Or, you, *señora*, do you feel capable of having the keys, or no?"

"Well, give me a chance, engineer. If you see that I am not capable of the work, just tell me, and I will give the keys back to you. But I feel badly that you took them away from her."

"No need to feel badly. She provoked it."

Well, from that day on, I was in charge of the personnel and of the warehouse, so that when any worker needed tools or some materials, they had to ask me for them and I wrote down what they had taken. And I gave a report every week to the engineer. Well now he did not even come for the report. He just arrived at about 9 in the morning. He greeted me and said he would see me in a while, and this while lasted until 5 in the afternoon, when we left work. He left the whole enchilada to me and said we would see each other in the afternoon. And if I was lacking any materials, like copper piping, I had to wait until the next day--because the infamous engineer did not show up any more. And in the afternoon, before leaving, I had to check the apartments and houses to see that the work was done well, and write down what was still needed.

And so it went with this work, but I liked it. And I had to supervise the women so that the dwellings were very clean, ready to surrender to their owners. I was in charge of a little more than a hundred dwellings. And I looked like a prison guard with all the keys I carried around. There were times that I needed the help of one of my workers, because there was so much to do. I left the warehouse to her in case anyone arrived to pick up some materials, so she could write down who and what and how much was taken, so that I could go and check each dwelling again in the morning. Because there were times that copper was stolen at night, and the copper had to be replaced. And the guards didn't even notice. Either they stole it or maybe they were in accord with the robbers who gave them their cut. Well, all this was a loss for the company.

And I also had to make sure the workers were working. Because there were occasions when I didn't hear a sound in the dwellings. I went and looked and nothing. But when I found them they were inside a house smoking their marijuana cigarette, women as well as men. I found out because it looked like smoke from a bonfire. And I myself got high from breathing the smoke. Better to leave and see if the engineer found them. They weren't even worried. For me, as long as they did the work well, I would leave them to it. A taco seller also entered the condominiums to make a sale, and I let them eat.

One day the engineer surprised us when they were happily eating away. And he said to me, "*Señora*, why aren't they working? Who let them eat at this hour?"

And I answered him, "Engineer, a worker who does not eat hasn't the strength to work."

And he said to me, "Well, *señora*, I´ll see you in the afternoon."

"What, you are not going to return?"

"Why should I return? You are in command here. Just so they do the work well."

"And when has it not been done well?"

"I know. For this reason I trust you."

"Well, many thanks for your trust. But don't leave me alone for so long!"

"*Señora*, I ask you that if someone comes, you give them a list of the workers. They are going to come from the Social Security (IMSS, *Instituto Mexicano de Seguro Social*, Mexican Institute of Social Security, which handles medical care and pensions for formal sector workers) and you are in charge of giving them the list."

And that was the way it was when I was working for this company. I only worked about two months with the other women, and then was given the keys to the houses and condominiums. It meant greater responsibility, but the work was less physically difficult.

I kept this work for almost a year, but bit-by-bit it was being completed. And before they laid me off, a friend of mine, a neighbor, proposed to me that I go to clean houses with her in El Centro, California [about 12 miles from the Mexicali-Calexico border]--that they needed women to clean houses. And I told her, yes, but that I would have to quit my job first. And so I did.

The engineer didn't want me to leave. He said that there was going to be work in other housing developments and that he had me on the list of those who were going to be employed. But I didn't want to and I said that I thanked him but that I had another job. I didn't tell him where, but he told me I had been very responsible, and in any case, whenever I wished to return he would have work for me. I thanked him and went to say goodbye to all the workers. And the women told me that I was leaving as a "slave driver." Because that is the name they gave me. They said I treated them like slaves.

But they said it as a joke, because I kept them working and never left them alone. But that was my job. Because if I didn't do it the made the fool and didn't get on with the work. And I had to get at least five dwellings cleaned between 8 in the morning and 5 in the afternoon--and very clean. Because if not I had to have them clean them again. And there, with the salary they earned, they were paid very well. They were very content and very thankful to me since even this I had got for them. I spoke to the engineer, asking him to raise the salary, so that they would do better work. This engineer was of good character. We liked the way he treated us, but he was very strict as far as the work went. He came from Puebla and knew how to handle people.

[She left this work partially because of the many robberies. One of the boys from the colonia was among the thieves, and she was afraid that if they caught him, he would say that she, too, was stealing.]

And so I began to work in the United States, through the help of a friend. The first job was in El Centro, California. I cleaned silverware because it was all the *señora* was able to save when her house burned down. She didn't know how to clean it, and I helped her and told her what to by, and she did so. She was very grateful for how I cleaned it. And she gave me the pieces that couldn't be cleaned. And so I began my work there.

Afterwards she invited me to go to San Diego to clean her house there once a week and she would find me work the other days of the week, recommend me to her friends, so that I had a full week's work. And I could sleep at her house. And wherever I worked I could go to Mexicali or to Rosarito, where I also have family, on the weekends. [This woman paid Ernestina $20 a day for cleaning her house. A decade earlier, $40 to $45 dollars a day was the norm.]

I took this decision so as not to be close to the house because of everything that had happened to me with the adulterers. And I, of necessity, had to pass by the house where that woman had lived and it made me very angry. She lived on the same street, a few houses down. Because of this I withdrew for some time until the rancor or feelings dissipated. Because being in the house was not good for me even if I worked. And there—San Diego—I forgot about it a little. But coming back to or being in the house caused me nostalgia. Because whether one's husband has been good or bad, you always feel an emptiness in the surroundings

And what I did was to arrive at my house and begin cleaning it while I played music to distract me a little. The worst thing that was happening to me was that I was beginning to like to drink beer every day. And this was not good because it provoked memories and I started crying. And my children were suffering upon seeing me in that state. They couldn't talk to me because I answered them nastily or I shouted at them. And they were not used to me yelling at them, even though they were older. I feel and believe that I was becoming an alcoholic and if I didn't react in time I was going to spoil my life and the lives of my children, they just seeing how I was so depressed.

I didn't care what people thought of me. At first I did not want to go out on the street because I felt the people looked at me and criticized me. I don't doubt that some gossips did so, but I myself said, "Ernestina, it very bad what you are doing!" And thus I demonstrated to myself that I could succeed without anyone's help and that I was a woman of worth. Because this is what my parents taught me, the moral value of saying "I come because I can, and if I don't come, let's see if I can" (*"yo vengo porque puedo, y si no vengo, a ver si puedo."*)

I never forget those, my father's words. I also remember that he said to me, "If they ask you, my daughter, what can you do, you tell them 'Anything I need to do.' If you do not know how to do it, make the effort and do it anyway. He told me this in his own words, like rural-dwellers express themselves. All these words stayed in my mind and the moment arrived to apply what my father said to me.

My children now were worried because of the state they saw me in. And I heard them say among themselves, "Now my mama should not worry. Now my papa left. Better. Now we are more tranquil without having him yelling at us and cursing."

All this that I am commenting upon, was to get rid of the depression I felt. Fortunately, now they are only memories. And now I laugh about those memories and I speak very seriously to all of my children. And they remember how I was acting. But I tell them they should forget everything—now many years have passed. That thanks to God we are better off now.

I also remember times when I arrived from work. I now had an embargo order from one of the newspapers that by then I had nothing to do with. My husband was the one who sold them. But it was after he had left the house. I never knew that he had also left debts with the press. It happened that they returned one day with a lawyer saying there was a 40,000 peso debt. It was logical that it worried me, at the same time that it made me very angry. Not with the lawyer, but with my husband who had left us this debt as well. We had just paid back the suppliers of the motor oils, and another debt appears.

The truth is that I was afraid they would seize the only patrimony we had, which was the house, and that we would still be in debt. But I gathered my courage and said to the lawyer that I did not owe the press anything. I was almost completely convinced that nothing was owed. And I asked the lawyer to give me a copy of the bill, to see when it was dated. And since I have always been very careful to keep receipts--even though my husband threw them out, saying he didn't want to accumulate trash--I always retrieved them from the garbage pail, as I continue to do when my children throw out a doubled up paper, and I revise it and save it.

171

And they did give me a copy of the bill, but it wasn't marked as paid. Well, I got even more nervous and I say, may God now do what is destined for us. And I went about looking for the famous bill. And it was the same, unpaid. And I was even more frightened. During those days I didn't even go to work, expecting them to arrive and take everything away from me. But I, persistent, looked among all those papers I had saved. And what was my surprise, it was not among those papers but in the glove compartment of the car, because I almost dismantled the car looking for any proof. And if the receipt wasn't there I still had the bill saying it had not been paid. But the invoice was there, giving the quantity and the date that coincided with the bill they had brought. And thanks to God, I proved that nothing was owed.

But then I saw my house empty or simply me without a house. I remained hopeful that the only thing my husband had in his name was the car. And these were the things my children and I were remembering. The newspaper that wanted to charge us was called *Novedades*. Now it is called *La Crónica*.

Well, these *señores* came, together with the lawyer, asking my pardon, saying maybe they forgot to sign the invoice that they had brought, and they had finished their work. But what would have happened if the receipt had not been in the car, if in one of Adolfo's outbursts or crazy moments he had thrown out everything and I was not aware of it? And I had to living paying it off? But thanks to God I have had the strength to continue living and fighting for my future, and, above all, for my family. The good thing is that almost always, and up to now, I am aware of what is happening at home and can save the situation no matter how difficult it becomes.

Before the problem with *La Crónica* there had been a similar problem in the past with another newspaper, *La Voz*. The children who sold the newspaper for us, and we ourselves as well, were waiting for the newspapers to be delivered to us, because in the beginning the press distributed them at the house. And nothing arrived. We were waiting for 3 days and didn't know why. But since we sold *La Crónica* (previously called *Novedades*) and the weekly paper, *Zeta*, we vended those. And the accountant for the press came to bill my husband for a debt he supposedly owed for a week of selling *La Voz*—500 newspapers daily. But the strange thing is that since we had started to vend it, they had never come to the house to get the money. Almost always, as soon as we finished selling we counted up the earnings and went to the press to pay them. Because Adolfo was an independent seller who had to go to pay immediately, so they would bring us more newspapers to the house the following day. And they didn't bring them for several days. And it seemed strange to my husband but still he did not go to see what had happened. But it turned out that we supposedly owed this debt. I don't know for how much it was. That's because I also don't remember how much the newspaper sold for at this time. All they paid us was 30 percent for each newspaper sold.

The situation was that Adolfo had also thrown these receipts into the garbage, because, according to him, since the bills were now paid, why did one want so many receipts, and he put himself to throwing them away in the garbage can. Well, he went around very worried looking for the famous garbage bag that he had thrown in the trash and asking me, "Ernestina, did you by any chance retrieve the bag with the receipts? Let's see if it has the invoice they gave me at the press. I don't remember where I left it. And if I don't find it I am screwed. How am I going to prove that the newspapers are paid for?"

Well, I went to look for the famous garbage bag. I found it and gave it to him and said, "Now see. You all, and primarily you, criticize me, saying that I am like a pack rat, that I have junk all over the place. Here it is."

And he went to work to look for the famous invoice. Well, he found it immediately. He went to show them that he did not owe them anything. They saw the invoice. They compared the dates with the bill the press had. But they didn't have the receipt because it turned out that the accountant hand not turned in the money to the accounting office. He had saved it to pay the bills of another person who was also a vendor, but in a stall selling magazines.

Well, so as not to make the story long, they compared payments and it seems that the press owed Adolfo, because on the invoice they had given him, it showed that he had paid more than he owed, and so they started delivering newspapers to him again. And when he came home from the press he was very content. But if I hadn't been a pack rat, as he called me, they would have billed him again and he would have had to pay it because he had no proof of payment.

Because of this, whenever I see a paper thrown on the floor, I always pick it up and read it, and if it is important I save it. Also, a number of times and up until now, I was sure that my children had paid for some raffle tickets from the university that they gave them to sell. And the same thing happened. A representative from the university came by and said the owed the amount of 390 pesos for ten tickets and they wanted it now because another raffle was going to begin and they wanted to close the accounts on this one. Well, I angrily called my son and scolded him in front of the representative. And my son was surprised, arguing that these tickets had already been paid for.

That was when he said to me, that according to him, he had given me the receipt to save. But he had only come home and told me that now he had paid for the tickets-- he never gave me the sales slip. But he insisted he had given it to me to save. And it wasn't like that. He thought or believed this, but I think that when he took out his wallet from his pocket, it fell out. And I picked it up and gave it to the representative.

And it was true that all of the tickets had been paid for. But the fool had not signed it. And the good thing was that the receipt Guillermo had was stamped as paid, and the copy the *señor* had did not have that stamp. Perhaps they gave him another invoice. But all was cleared up right then. And I said to the representative, "Here you have the stamped sales slip." Perhaps it had not been handed into the accounting office as paid. Everything was cleared up, everything. But if I don't go around picking up what they throw away, they would have to pay for all of this again.

I don't have a good memory because I don't remember where I leave things. But I do remember if they give me something to save, even if I have to go about looking for it all day. But I find it. Or I simply stop looking for it for a good while until without thinking and without looking, I find it.

Perhaps none of this makes sense for me to comment upon, but for me they are details though which we have lived, and for me they are important to remember. It was not so easy to have a family or to take care of eight children. And each child thinks and acts differently. And what is more difficult is a husband who does not understand reason. All of this worries one as a mother. One believes that upon marriage, each one will handle his or her own problems, but it is not like that. The children grow, and the problems grow--because it is no longer them alone. Now the daughter-in-law and the grandchildren are involved. Fortunately, I have never had problems with them. I don't take part in the problems. They are problems that they, as a married couple, have to resolve. And so it has been. I take care of the single ones who have remained at home. There are enough problems with them. [At the time Ernestina wrote this portion of her book, her youngest son, Guillermo (Memo) and third eldest son, Marcelo, were living at home. Later on in the year Marcelo moved out and started living with his girlfriend.]

Chapter 10. My Daughters and Sons

I am thankful that Adolfo is gone because now I can make decisions and manage for myself and feel that I am and was worth something for my children. It is a very sad life to be living with someone and feel like one is worth zero to him, and he not taking into account what one does as a wife. What he does or not do away from the family nucleus now does not matter to me, given that he now has another family—even though he has never had children with the other woman, because she could not have more children, just those she had with her husband.

What comforts me is that is spite of the fact that he was a womanizer like the typical Mexican *macho*, I was married to him and no other woman that he has had who gave him children had legitimate children, as I have, because none of the other children has his surname. It is not something to be proud of because they did not ask to be born and not have his surname, and my children do.

I talk to my offspring about these children--or better youth--because it is best to do so. There have been cases that without knowing about each other they come to have a romantic relationship and even marry, and then the problems start. Because of this I tell my children clearly. All this hurts me, but it is better. I don't know if their mothers have told their own children, but that is their problem.

The only thing is that I got rid of him and now I am free and can leave my house without asking permission. I just inform my children so that they know where I am going and with whom. Now I have a pension from the years I worked at the trucking warehouse. I don't receive much from Social Security (I.M.S.S.), but I am happy.

I have a long-time friend who once lived in the colonia in Mexicali, who invites me to visit her at her house in Los Cabos. I have accompanied her to conferences in various parts of the United States, and we have gone to Taxco, Guerrero together. I go to visit my family as often as I can, to my son in Rosarito, B.C., to my daughter in Phoenix. I go to visit my hometown in Chihuahua.

Maybe some people will say I exaggerate, but it is very frustrating to stay with someone under these conditions and everything because he does not want to talk, or not have a trusted person to listen to you and be discrete.

I would not want the same thing that happened to me to happen to other woman, and everything because of not speaking up. Maybe worse things are happening to them than happened to me. But this happens to us because of not having communication with anyone. We suffer the same: physical and psychological mistreatment, some more than others. But the only thing that makes us different is that some endure more than others.

Before we said, "I have to put up with it because he is the father of my children and I do not want them to one day protest to me about anything." And now they do not put up with it, because they say, "I don't have to put up with anything. I can succeed alone and before he hits me I´ll leave him and find work. For this there are many *maquiladoras* or in some way I have to support my children." And the time of our predecessors is over, when women endured many things from their men. I was one of them, because I feared what people would say and we women are singled out because the men were not going to admit they were guilty. They would conveniently say that for some reason this is happening, referring to us being unfaithful or not.

We took care of them as they deserved to be taken care of, but this was years ago. I believe the same thing happened to my eldest daughter that happened to me. She was among those who said, "I have to put up with him because he was that way when I met him, and furthermore, he is the father of my children and I am a one-man woman." To the degree of putting up with him when she was pregnant with their second child, and my son-in-law went around drunk. He told her that the child she was going to have was not his, and that he didn't want her to have it.

I got very angry and said to my daughter that she not put up with him, that she separate from him, and that she take note of what happened to me at her father's side. Well the moment of birth arrived, and that day my son-in-law decided to go to Arizona, and he left her hanging as concerns the child. Well, I saw my own case in my daughter, and I was surprised that it happened in spite of the fact that she was well schooled—she was studying pedagogy in a rural teachers' training school. And even so she clung to him, well, until she saw that he didn't even send her money. He had said that the baby was not his baby, but he had an older daughter that he adored. He didn't send her anything either. And after she weaned the little boy, my daughter had to find work to feed her children.

The good thing was that she had returned and was living at home during the time she was working, and I took care of the children for her. Until one day, when the boy was three years old, my son-in-law telephoned my daughter saying that he was going to send her money to pay a *coyote* [people smuggler] and cross over. That he was going to be waiting for her in Phoenix. But I told her to think carefully about what she was going to do. That it was not easy to go because she was going to cross the border with children, a boy of three and the girl aged eight. And that she had not heard from him in three years.

But she did not listen to me. She went around looking for a *coyote*, who would charge her 3,000 dollars. Fortunately, a neighborhood friend recommended one to her and took her to meet him. And she crossed jumping the fence and walking, and the children passed with birth certificates of children the same age. But my daughter did not figure on the fact that when she arrived, her husband was living with another woman. And it was a hard blow, because he wanted to keep her in the same house as the other woman, arguing that she was only a friend and a workmate. But as my daughter told me, "Mamá, what chance would there be that she spoke with such confidence, and the children of this woman called him papa? And she was pregnant and without a husband. That day he took me to that house and the next day I made him rent an apartment for me and didn't let him stay with me. I took my children."

"And, *gorda*, what did you do the night you arrived?"

"Mama, I felt like a crushed cockroach, but what could I do? But as soon as he woke up he left and the came back with his dumbbell face and took me to the apartment. I believe he already had everything planned because he didn't want to leave me but neither did he want to leave that woman. And he later told me clearly that the child that that woman was going to have was his. And I told him that if he wanted to see his children he could come by, but stay outside, because I was never going to let him come inside the apartment. And I told him he was going to have to pay the rent and give me money for my children.

"Ay, mama, if you could see how I suffered, with so much anger, and coming to a place where I knew no one. Well, he did pay the rent for the first three months, but he did not bring me money to buy food for the children. Necessity drove me to look for work, leaving the children with a neighbor who offered to take care of them for me. And Nadia [her daughter] began to be rebellious, because she wanted to go to live with her papa."

"What happened?"

"Well, I had to call Juan so he would take her with him, and he did so. But she didn't stay because the children of his old lady hit her, and the fat one [Juan] accepted it, because he said she was not his. Ay mamá, he is their father."

179

"Yes, I know. And now that she is growing up, the more she looks like him. I hope she does not follow in her father's footsteps. And, *gorda*, have you seen the boy the other woman had?"

"Yes. He also looks a lot like Juan.

"One day when the other woman was still pregnant, she came to my apartment to fight with me, saying that she didn't want me to be asking Juan for money for my children. If you could see how angry I became because of her coming to shout at me in my own home! And I grabbed her by the hair and slapped her, saying that it had been some time since I hadn't received even a dollar from Juan. I think he spent money getting drunk and told her he was giving it to me.

"I began cleaning houses because he stopped giving me money, and she complains. I believe she was going to bring a lawsuit against me. But since it was she who came to bother me, she must have thought it over and she didn't do anything. But she left with her tail between her legs when I told her I had left him and she should go bother him, and that I did not want to see her again."

And thus it was that my eldest daughter began to struggle in a place she did not know, to support my grandchildren. She has always been a warrior. Circumstances have let her get ahead, cleaning houses, crocheting clothes, making decorations for *quinceañeras* and brides, even drawing pictures of movie stars and selling them. Thanks to all of this she has been able to bring up her children, giving them an education. And as she says, "I work to give a better life to my children, for everything their father has not given them."

I found out that the rumor is that he was deported and now is in Chihuahua. Because that is where my ex-son-in-law is from. He stayed neither with my daughter nor with the other woman. And all this happened because he was a drunk and irresponsible with his family.

In truth I do not know how my daughter does it, with all the obligations she has. She is even a soccer player. With all the work she has, she goes to the soccer field to play soccer. But she has always loved sports and she has her children on a soccer team. And in the evenings after school she takes them for practice. And she takes them to music classes as well. She is a woman who has much energy, despite her 44 years.

In the final analysis, when I ask her about Juan, she says that according to her mother-in-law he is out of control and she believes that he is not only getting drunk but also uses drugs. My daughter still maintains a relationship with her mother-in-law who visits her to see my grandchildren. Unfortunately, my daughter was very much in love with him, but when finding out everything, this love was converted into anger and enmity.

Now she has a relationship with another man, who is the father of her two youngest children, both born in the United States. He treats her well and cares about her two other children. But she told me, "I speak clearly to him." She told him about the problems she had had and that if he wanted to be with her there were conditions, like helping her pay for what was spent in the house, and that she didn't want him becoming jealous or anything similar, and that she liked to take the children out to eat, and go out once in a while to hear musical groups. If he did not want to accompany her she would go with a female friend of hers and she would look for someone to take care of the children. And so they agreed. The young man already knew her. He had a lot of respect for me and for my grandchildren. He cares a lot about her. His name is Adrián Pérez. He is from Coahuila, from the city of Torreón.

One of the things that bother me is that my daughters did not finish their degrees as teachers, neither of them, Indira or Magali, because of marrying these worthless men. I cried a lot when I found out that Magali had left with her boyfriend, when she was in the middle of her studies. Because she ran away with her boyfriend the day after she had been elected queen of the rural teachers' training school of Cuidad Saucilllo, Chihuahua. And this. after all their efforts to get permission from their father to let them attend.

It was me who looked schools for teachers and I went to SEP (*Secretaría de Educación Pública*, Secretariat of Public Education) in Mexicali. And fortunately they guided me, asking where I was from and I told them where. And I told them about the situation in which we found ourselves and that the girls wished to study, but it shouldn't be very expensive. Well, the secretary of SE. told me that precisely in the town where I was from there was a woman's teachers school and it would be convenient for me to send them there because the federal government would give them scholarships and it wouldn't cost me anything except for their transportation there and their personal effects.

And thus they went--or better said--I took them. The school accepted them gladly. Their schoolmates esteemed them a lot. And more, they were the only ones in any school generation to have come from Baja California to study there. And since they lived in the dormitory, there was no lack of schoolmates from their group who would take them home on weekends--because almost all of their schoolmates were from nearby *ranchos*. And they were fascinated, my poor daughters, who had never gone alone anywhere before. Even though they were at the preparatory school level, they were still very naïve. And the kids they hung out with were from *ranchos* and their fathers also didn't let them go out. The kids taught them to pick chilies, tomatoes, and knock down walnuts from the trees. Their schoolmates' parents taught my daughters to milk cows and how to prepare the milk to make cheese. And if they and their friends were invited to some dance on some rancho, their friends' parents took them and then went to pick them up.

Magali told me that when they had spent the little money I sent them, Indira would tell her, "I'll be back soon," and then she grabbed her bag where she had her hair cutting apparatus, and walked street by street through the village of Saucillo, offering to cut hair. And when she returned she would give half of the money she had earned to Magali, and they would go to buy their personal effects. . This was when they stayed in the dormitory during the weekends and did not wish to accompany their schoolmates to their homes. Or they also went to the fields where they were needed to pick chilies and they learned to process them to make chipotle

Later on some first cousins of mine took my daughters to live with them on weekends, and I am very grateful to them for the attention they paid to my daughters. One of them has passed on. Mauro Ibarbol López, may he rest in peace. The other cousin and his wife moved to Ciudad Juárez as soon as his daughter, a classmate of my daughters, graduated.

I was more preoccupied with Magali, because she was a bit shyer than Indira. And because of this things happened to her that I did not wish to happen--that the first man that talked to them nicely made them enthusiastic. And so it happened. Cadgers were not lacking to make them fall in love and at first sight my daughters went away with them and stopped studying. I felt very disappointed with them because they left their careers unfinished. And they didn't know how to value the sacrifices I had made for them, or, at the same time, the needs they suffered without being able to even buy a soda to drink. Because sacrifices are always needed if you wish to exit from ignorance.

And everything in order to follow after men that later made them suffer, as also happened to Magali.

Magali fell in love with her Prince Charming, who later became her worst nightmare. At the beginning, as she herself told me, "Mamá, I swear that nothing is lacking at home. He takes me out everywhere. He opened a bank account for me so that I could make use of the money and buy whatever I needed. He bought me all new furniture and I did not have to remind him when the monthly rent was due. He was responsible about everything. He even bought me a house so that we did not have to pay rent. He took me out dining, and I had no problems with him.

"When I got pregnant with Cristina, he took me to the clinic every month for check-ups. And of course I took care of him as the wife I was. When he came home from work, I had his dinner prepared and had his clothing ready so he could shower. I shined his boots. Mama, as far as I was concerned, everything was perfect, because he always returned home early. When he didn't want to dine at home he took me out to a restaurant. When he arrived from work, I took off his boots so he could rest. And he told me when he had to work overtime.

"And when Cristina was about to be born, he bought her a crib. We went to buy baby clothes—we knew the baby was a girl. In one word, I never noticed anything wrong. And I so naïve never suspected anything about what was going on because he took such good care of me. He took me to visit his parents. But my mother-in-law didn't like me or she resented that I had taken away her baby, who was her spoiled child. That is what I felt. But little by little I was winning her over, and she let me know many things that I had not noticed. And she said to me, 'Magali, take care with René—that he does not become crafty.' But I didn't even pay attention to what she said

184

to me. I asked myself why she would say this to me if I did not notice anything crafty about him. He always came home early and did not go out.

"And that is how it went, mama. And when my skinny one was born, he took off work to take care of me. He was very pleased. He took good care of the little girl. And she grew until she reached the age of one. And we had a party for her first birthday. My husband invited his workmates, even his boss, the chief inspector of the packaging plant."

Because Magali's husband was an accountant and he earned very well according to what she said—I didn't have much time to get together with them. She told me she heard her husband's boss say, "What a pretty wife you have. She doesn't deserve what you are doing."

"But I still didn't understand what he meant. I continued taking care of the man as always. What a moron I was. Mama, when Cristina was a year and a half old, he came home from work and told me to pack his suitcase because the plant was sending him to work in Monterrey for three days. And the big moron put herself to packing his suitcase for his trip. And when he returned and went to work, I unpacked his dirty clothes to wash them. But what was my surprise when I felt something in one of his pants' pockets. And I took out the receipts. He wasn't in Monterrey, but in Acapulco. And the trip tickets were for the day he had gone. And it wasn't one ticket but two, one with the name of a woman, and a receipt for the hotel. The fool had forgotten them in the pocket of his pants.

"And even so, I did not grasp anything. I put the receipts away until he would ask for them. But days passed and I began to have doubts. And once again he took me to visit my mother-in-law and I asked her why she had said that I should be careful with her son. And it was then she said that it seemed—but I should talk to him first and see what he says—that he was going around with a woman who was from Acapulco. And it was then that I understood the airline tickets. And what I did, mama, was to remain silent—not say anything to my mother-in-law. I picked up Christina and went home, gathered together my clothing and my little girl's, and when René arrived I gave him the tickets. And I swear, mama, that I didn't know whether to hit him and get rid of my anger, or to break down crying.

"I felt that my idol had turned to dust. It was as though I had been blindfolded. And worse yet when he told me that he had married her, but didn't want to leave me. Mama, the shameless man wanted to live with both of us. Because the other woman was pregnant by him, mama. But I asked myself, when had all this occurred if I never noticed anything?"

"Ay, Magali. It happened when he told you he must remain late to work overtime, but was with her. And you so believing in what he told you, just so you would not suspect anything. And then when his boss told him that you did not deserve that he was cheating on you, you didn't even wake up because of the blindfold you had over your eyes. And you, what did you do?"

"The only thing I did was to tell him that I was going to Mexicali to be with you, and that I was taking the little girl. I left everything to him. I just went to *la gorda* (Indira) and told her I was going to go to be with you because I had left René and was returning to Mexicali. And I asked her if she could go for the furniture and sell it for me so she could send me a bit of money. And believe me, mama, he was still so cynical that he took me to the bus station. He believed I was going to repent. But I had made my decision. The page had been turned. And the rest, mama, you know what happened—when he tried to kidnap Cristina.

"And you and Maria Mora and all of my siblings' friends acted like detectives. Better yet, you looked like spies from the anti-kidnapping squad in Cachanilla. Now I laugh about everything that happened. Now, thank God, I have overcome this. And you see that since I entered the *maquiladora* as an operator and later became line supervisor, I have supported myself for 20 years."

But Magali had to endure all these problems so she would find out that you cannot live in a fantasy world. And after this experience she had another one with her second husband. She did not learn. She looked for another problem with a young man from the colonia where we live. He was the father of her second child, a daughter as well. I think this was even worse because he didn't even have formal or stable work. And he would tell her to make him a packaged lunch to take to work, and when he guessed that Magali had gone, he returned and ate the tacos in the house, and then disappeared again until she came home from work. Then he presented himself and though he had just returned from work, and she very credulous.

But the strange thing is, he gave Magali her weekly allowance. We don't know if he borrowed the money or if he was involved in something else. Until little by little she found out that he did not work and she began to notice that he came home drugged. And she also left the other little girl in his care. But fortunately she was now with the mother who always has bailed her children out from many problems. And I would not dare to leave them without help, both my sons and my daughters, because I wouldn't want the same things to happen to them as happened to me. That because of not having any family nearby, their father could do to me what he wished. I had neither voice nor vote in the house. I took care of all of them when I could. I have been like a second mother to my grandchildren.

Until she married I took my eldest granddaughter (Cristina) with me to visit my sons who lived outside of Mexicali. [One son lives in Rosarito, another in Calexico, California]. But after marrying she continued studying with the help of Magali, her mother. Cristina has been a very intelligent kid in her studies since kindergarten. She has many first-place certificates and now she is going to graduate in pedagogy from the university (U.A.B.C., *Universidad Aútonoma de Baja California*). And the younger one, Karla, is going along the same path. She is not as studious, but she does try hard. There is 5 years of difference between her and Cristina.

Maybe Magali feels guilty about having deserted her career, and feels obligated to help Cristina. Because even though Cristina is living with her husband, Magali is paying for her university. Because Cristina's husband is currently studying psychology and working as a librarian in a secondary school to help out with the expenses for the little boy they have. Cristina's husband's parents are also helping him along in his career. Almost all of his family are teachers and want him to get his degree. The good thing is that both Magali and Cristina's husband's parents, are helping them out.

Magali now has a new relationship and it looks like things are going well with him. At least they have spent a longer time together, though she has not had children with him, because she had her tubes tied after her second daughter was born. But I think that she put her cards on the table, telling him she did not want the same things to happen as happened with the fathers of her two daughters. She told him that she didn't want another failure.

I, to tell the truth, did not like him at first, because it seemed to me he would not last with Magali, because he was very jealous of her and he was also quite a drinker. But Magali gave him the option, "Or stop drinking, or leave the house. I don't want a bad example for my daughters. You decide, because we have talked, and you do not listen. So either you sort yourself out or you sort yourself out. In the final analysis, I was not born with a man at my side."

And that is how he stopped drinking. Now he does not drink a drop of alcohol. He behaves super well. Anything I need he does for me. He esteems me a lot. I also esteem him and not because he does things for me, but simply because he cares a lot about my granddaughters and my great-grandson (Christina's son). They love him very much because for them he is their father and grandfather. I pamper him as well because when he and Magali finish work they come to my house every day. I make the food she likes for my granddaughter Karla, who is in secondary school, even though Magali gets angry and says, "Ay, mama, don't spoil her so much."

"It isn't that I am spoiling her. Simply put, if she behaves well with me, she behaves well with you."

Magali is now the person who runs the household and the truth is that I tell her not to be so hard on her husband, because he is going to get fed up and might leave. And what she answers is, "If he wants to go, the doorway is very broad." Because she knows he will not leave. She has been with Juan for 11 years.

My granddaughter Karla treats him as though he were her papa, even knowing her biological papa lives close by. But she says her papa is Juan, because if she meets her real father on the street, he just nods in greeting, and she returns to the house very sad. I am very sorry for her because we never hid who her real papa was from her. Her aunts and uncles do greet her, and they love her a lot because she is their brother's only daughter.

Aida is the youngest of my daughters, even though she was older than they were when she married. She was always the most fragile and emotional, but she never let her arm be twisted. She studied electronic technology. She was overprotected by her

189

siblings. But when her sisters left, the separation hurt her. Even though she was very quiet about it, I saw that she missed them terribly. But she didn't say anything to me. She became very lonely. But when she graduated from secondary school she wanted to go to the teachers' training school along with her sisters. But I didn't let her. I told her that if she wished to continue studying she should look for a technical career. And so it was. She enrolled in a technical high school to study in the evenings and in the morning she worked as a cashier in a store. Fortunately, they let her work part time.

But afterwards, she began to go out alone. She looked for any pretext to go out. And her siblings acted as accomplices and they took her to the *antros*, once called discotheques, to dance. But this, yes, she did not stop studying. But what I didn't like was that she began to arrive later from the preparatory school with the pretext that she was staying to study with a group of students. And it seems she was seeing a boyfriend some place. And her siblings knew she had become the girlfriend of one of their friends. And worse, the boyfriend she acquired was older—5 years older than her. He was the eldest in the group of friends. Well, I stopped it immediately. But she continued to see him secretly. And I was confident that she was not seeing him. But she found some way to see him.

And the strange thing was that she began sleeping a lot and didn't want to go to school. And then Indira commented to me—because Indira had not yet gone to Phoenix—"Listen, mamá, it seems to me that Aida is pregnant." And I, still doubtful, said, "I don't believe so, because she is not anyone's girlfriend."

And when I said that, Indira started laughing. "Mamá, look at her face. It is very pale and furthermore her belly is growing. Why do you think she goes around in loose blouses and wanting to vomit? It's just that you haven't found out. All of us know."

The only thing I did was to ask Aida to bring her boyfriend so I could talk to him. I couldn't do anything else, given that she was no longer a minor. It was something I had not expected with Aida, because I saw her as being too delicate to have done such a foolish thing. Maybe I was partially guilty about what happened, because when the father of my children was still with us, it occurred to Aida to say in front of us both, "Mama, I am never going to get married."

And I turned to look at her and said jokingly, "You're not going to marry because I am going to put you in a convent and you will become a nun."

And she began laughing and said to me, "I will never marry, but I am going to have a child. I want to be a mama."

"That's fine Aida. Have your child and I will take care of you."

And her papa turned to me and said, "What good advice you are giving her instead of scolding her. Better that she sets herself to studying or to working. " And we both broke out laughing upon seeing his reaction.

And that's how everything was. We did not return to the subject again. And then I came to see that it was true what she had said that day. And that is what was left for me to say to her, "This is what you had planned. But now you are screwed. Go and tell this good for nothing that I want to talk to him. That he come and face me, and right now. Let's see what he has to say."

My anger was so great that the only thing I did was to break down crying and to say to Aida, "You see what happened to your sisters and you didn't react. And I want to see him right now." She got up, sleepy as she was, and went to his house to fetch him. I don't know what she said to him. The matter was that they arrived, and he with his tail between his legs and a nervous smile, without knowing what to say. And I waiting for him to speak.

And in the end he got the courage to say, "Well, I love your daughter and I want to marry her. We have talked about this."

"Oh yes? When do you plan to get married? When the little creature is born? Do you have a place to live? Because Aida has a place to sleep, however poor it may be. And you as a man, and older than she is, do you have your own means to live and are you offering her something worthwhile? Because if you are going to put her in your parents' house as often happens, we have begun on the wrong foot. And she, in the state she is in, has to be cared for. I do not oppose your marrying but I entrust you to treat her well--because here at home her siblings and I treat her well. I don't want to learn that you touch a hair on her head. Even though you are married, I will go and fetch her and everything she has in her belly."

That is how I gave my point of view. "Now it is your turn to say something, and I want you to be clear about one thing. I do not like it at all that you have gotten ahead of yourselves and left her pregnant. The truth is I don't know what you do, whether you are working or have a profession. I only know you live in Colonia Satélite and are a friend of my sons. That's all I know about you. Now it's your turn to talk."

I was anxious for him to say something. But he hadn't a word to say. He just turned to look at Aida, very nervous, and then looked at everyone who was by my side. My other children were there along with some of their friends, because as soon as they knew that he was coming to talk to me they made an agreement to be present, so that they could tease him about it afterwards.

But Aida, very sure of herself, told him, "It's your turn to say something, or is it that you are not going to talk?"

"Well, I studied to be an electronics technician and that is what I am working as. My papa has a workshop downtown and I help him repair all kinds of electrical equipment. Because he is well along in age he needs someone to help him out. And he doesn't want to employ anyone outside of the family. And I earn well, enough to support your daughter. She and I have already talked about this."

"And so? When did you think of coming to talk to me? Is it that I count for nothing? And does your mama know about this? Because I imagine that you have told her you are going to marry. And where do you plan to live, in your house? Or when are you going to rent a house?"

"It's that I told Aida that we are going to live in my house up until the baby is born."

"And your papa, what did he say?"

"He doesn't know anything. He separated from my mama many years ago. And I am going to go and tell my mama right now. And I am going to bring her here so you get to know her."

"What interests me at the moment is you two. We'll see about the rest. Where are you going to live and when do you plan to marry? And once you are married I will get to know, if you wish, all the sacred family."

"Well, we will marry in two months, if you permit it."

"Well, it seems to me too long from now. The sooner the better. How does one month from now sound to you? And you must leave your house as soon as possible because I don't like the idea that your mama might meddle in your lives. Because if so there are going to be problems with me. For this reason I don't interfere with my sons-in-law or daughters-in-law. Their problems are theirs. But if I see that my sons mistreat their wives, I am on my daughters-in-law's side. And the same thing I say to my sons-in-law. If I see my daughters treating their husbands badly, I put a stop to it and vice versa.

"Then prepare the papers. Tomorrow we will present ourselves at the civil registry so the give us an appointment. The sooner the better." Well, whether he wanted to go or not, we went the next day. We were in agreement, all of us happy and content—my offspring just observing, and their friends as well. It was all about my having the last word so that the wedding would take place.

The next day arrived. My daughter Indira was at the sewing machine, making Aida a maternity dress. All of us got up early and prepared breakfast for Aida, so that she would not be hungry. According to Indira, so that Aida would not faint because of being pregnant. Now it looked like they were going to marry that very day. But we were just going to present the papers, so they would give us an appointment. But there was a beautiful joy in the house, my daughter Indira measuring the little garment for her sister.

As I said before, they spoiled Aida a lot. Her siblings bought her bracelets, necklaces, all very fancy, because they liked the way she dressed. The fact is she looked like a gypsy, the way she dressed up. Her siblings bought her boots at the open market, second-hand ones, because they did not have enough for new "Dr. Martins." The thing is that they kept her dressed up and she let herself be pampered by her siblings. The case is I told them to stop making such a scandal because we were just going to the civil registry to put in a request for an appointment. And I asked Indira why she was making Aida a dress, and Indira said, "Mama, so my sister looks pretty!"

"The situation is that we are ready to go and the boyfriend has not shown up. The only thing missing is that he has repented. I will go and haul him along by the ears."

"Ay, mama," Indira says to me, "It is because what you were saying made him nervous. He is just assimilating it all at this moment."

"Well so it should be, because I put my cards on the table."

"Look, mama, here he is coming, very handsome."

"Well, he's better off for it."

And we were all getting ready to leave when the friends also arrived and I asked them where they were going. And they answered me, "We are going to accompany you as well. We all reached an agreement so as to see if it is true that they are going to get married. Because we cannot believe she caught him. We have never known him to have a girlfriend, and he so old." They said he was old because they were very much younger than him.

"Let's go then. Get in the pick-up wherever you can fit."

And so as not to draw the story out, we arrived at the civil registry. They collected the papers and gave the couple an appointment two weeks later, sooner than we expected. I almost believe that the civil registry was also in a hurry to marry them.

Two weeks passed and once again the same thing: Indira very early in front of the sewing machine sewing another little maternity suit. And I said to her, "Look here, *gorda*, we have other things to do, even if it is only to make snacks to celebrate. Because today we are going to meet the new family and we don't even know who they are. There will be time to get acquainted with them when we go to the civil registry. And what if the brother-in-law doesn't want to sign the marriage certificate as a witness. What a shameful thing for our family. For this reason I am going prepared. I'll get that shameless one. But I don't believe he has repented. If he doesn't land my daughter he will remain a lonely bachelor and Aida is still young even if she has a child. There will be no lack of someone who wants her. There are many single mothers in the world and they get married even if they have children."

Well, when we arrived the bridegroom was standing at the door of the civil registry waiting for the bride. And that was when I met his mama. She was a very submissive woman. And I had to introduce myself to her because the sweethearts—distracted by the anxieties of marrying--didn't introduce us. Then we signed the marriage certificate as direct relatives and witnesses.

Well it seemed to be a very quick wedding, but they were married. Almost all of the bridegroom's relatives arrived at my house and several people, trusted friends, who were invited. We served all of them until late at night, because we made a little dinner for friends of the groom and my offspring. They brought beer. My daughter Indira had already bought several bottles of cider without my knowing about it. That day we made *birria* [a goat dish in chili sauce, traditionally served at wedding parties]. We ate and put on music to dance to. We drank a toast to the bride and groom. And about midnight people began leaving. Everything was orderly.

The next day the bride left with her groom, everything fine. We organized a baby shower in Aida's mother-in-law's house. Everything went fine up until then. But then the little problems started, because my son-in-law began to be jealous of her. And I didn't like this, because in the beginning Aida came to visit me daily so as not to feel lonely, even though her mother-in-law was in the house. But her mother-in-law was very reserved, and did not converse with her. And he began to prohibit Aida from coming to see me. He told her that he didn't want other men to see her, because she was his alone. And since she had had a boyfriend in the colonia where we lived, he didn't want her to run across him.

He began to arrive home drunk, to such a degree that he would slap her. And she didn't tell me anything. Until one day she arrived with their little boy and a bag full of clothing and with her eyes red from crying. And I asked her, "What is the matter with you? Why were you crying?"

"I am coming to stay with you."

"What did Mundo do to you?"

"It's that, mama, I can no longer endure his jealousy. He doesn't want me to come to visit you anymore. He says he doesn't want men to look at me. He just wants to keep me secluded. He doesn't even want to go to work so as to have me by his side, just embracing me. It is exaggeratedly bad, mama. And if I say something he gets angry. And now he has begun to slap me."

"And what do you plan to do?"

"It's that I no longer want to be with him."

"Ay, daughter. The only thing lacking is that you have the same life as your sisters. And that he also say that the little boy is not his. Well, think it over. I will accept you and the boy here. But I don't want him coming her and convincing you to go back, because that is not our agreement. I spoke very clearly to him. Let him come to look for you, but let him come sober. That he not come drunk because if he does I will send for a patrol car. And I don't want you to go out."

Well the cynic came some days later to try to convince her to go back with him. But I invited him in and talked to him again. That he not come here drunk. And I told him also that Aida was going to stay with me and I didn't want him coming to bother her. And if he wanted to come, that he did not arrive drunk. That's what I did. But they were alone with the boy. I don't know how he convinced her, but she went back with him.

I didn't want to meddle in their affairs if that was Aida's decision. For a while they were supposedly fine. And she came more often to the house without any problems. He came along to accompany her. He went to work at home in the job he knows how to do. Things went along like that for a long time and then Aida gave me the news that she was pregnant once again. But she was very content with her pregnancy. And what worried me is that after two years of marriage and on the point of having another child, they continued living in the same house as his mama—even though she did not meddle with them at all and loved her grandson very much.

And I began believing they were going to stay in this house. And on one side I felt badly, because the *señora* was going to be left alone, because my son-in-law was the only one of her offspring who lived with her, and she was quite old. Her other children almost never visited her. And Aida continued visiting me daily. But Mundo, my son-in-law, also visited me. I began to esteem him, but his jealousy did not completely disappear. He kept annoying her. He began drinking again, but less, and now in the house while he was working. He began to get enough work fixing electrical apparatuses and now there was no need for him to go help his father in the downtown workshop. It closed down because his other brothers didn't want to help their father out. They were very angry with him because he left their mama for another woman. And my son-in-law preferred to work at home. But it was a sacrifice for Aida to have him there because he wanted to have her by his side all of the time.

And it was restful for her when she came to visit in the evenings. When we had some family gathering they came with their children—now they had two sons. But as soon as Mundo arrived he went out to buy beer and to drink it. But as he drank the second one he got very nagging with Aida, and I didn't like that. And he began to bother her and took her back to the house. Until then next time I put a stop to it and spoke to him again. But he acted as though I were crazy. And my boys began to defend their sister, to the degree that they exchanged blows with him.

I did not like that there were these fights between family members. And I told him that when he thought of getting drunk, better that he did not come to the house, but that he didn't prohibit Aida from visiting me. And all of the problems stemmed from his drunkenness. And my daughter came often with her stream of children, because now they weren't one or two—in the end she had four. And he didn't stop insulting Aida all because of his damned jealousies and the much beer he was drinking was beginning to do him harm. He arrived at the house so drunk that he didn't know what he was doing, and the only thing I said to Aida was not to go outside. And he began shouting at her form the street and pounding on the door until he got tired and went home. There were times he arrived all beat up, and I didn't know with whom he had been fighting.

One of many times, some guy beat him up so badly—almost in front of the house—that if people had no come and told us, he would have died. It was someone who hid behind his police uniform to carry out his misdeeds and to beat up others. And we went to lodge a complaint against that character, but they told us that if we did not have the number of the patrol car—so they could locate whoever was driving it—they could do nothing. But that day he was driving his own car and we didn't know the license number or model. We did know his first name—he was named José—but not his surname, and we couldn't do anything. We had to take my son-in-law to the Red Cross clinic.

Some time later, when my grandchildren had grown up, he got drunk again and hit Aida. But my grandchildren couldn't do anything. What they did was to come and take refuge in my house, including my oldest grandson, aged 17. And the same thing happened. Mundo, acting crazily, entered their house and began to shout at Aida and at my grandchildren. And they, out of respect, withdrew and came to my house. But then came the worst. He arrived shouting insults and throwing rocks at the door and kicking it. The good thing was that two of my sons were at home and saw what he was doing. They called the police and a patrol car came and took him away. He looked like a child having a tantrum, throwing himself down on the street and rolling around. And we—Aida, the grandchildren, and I—watched him from a window as he flung himself to the ground.

He was obsessed with Aida. And even more so when she began to work, because my grandchildren were growing up and work became scarce for him. Now he obsessed about how many men she had talked to. And I felt there was a sickness in his jealousy. Well, he was now prohibited from coming to my house until, as I said to Aida, he behaved correctly. I told me daughter that I did not dislike him, and I esteemed him, but I could not have him coming to the house to make a scandal. Because my sons now said that they were going to run him off if he came to the house drunk. That even they did not engage in scandalous behavior, and even less should he. Because of this they prefer not to drink. Now even his friends cannot bear him. I tell them it is fine that when it is very hot I will let them drink a few little cans of beer, because it doesn't do harm to anyone to drink in moderation. Because even I feel like drinking when it is very hot here in Mexicali. Because we drink and drink water, and it just distends our stomachs.

Well, it seems he is now behaving better with Aida—or she doesn't want to tell me. Because I ask her, "Listen, Aida, how is Mundo behaving? Does he still insult you?" But she doesn't say anything. Maybe he changed as the children grew up. Because the other day he was going to shout at me, and Kevin, my oldest grandson, came to my defense. Because this kid does not take anything.

But what Mundo says to Aida is, "How many men did you talk to?"

"Yes, mama but now I learned not to listen to him. Now I say to him, 'I am going to talk to many men today.'"

"And what does he say?"

"He just smiles at me. And you know what he says to me at times, 'My daughter [*mi hija*, a term of affection], I don't want any man to look at you because you are so very pretty and I am afraid you will leave me for another.' And I answer him, 'Don't be ridiculous. If I didn't fine someone else before when I was younger, less so now. Who is going to want me with so many kids. You are ridiculous.'

"No, mama, I am no longer the same, but that doesn't mean I don't respect him. Now when I say I have been invited to go on an outing, he says he will come with me. I tell him I only have enough for my ticket. Previously he would hit me on both sides. And so that he does not go around being ridiculous, I know how to take care of him. Even more so knowing how he is. He now knows that these outings we have in the factory are with women alone. And in the area where I work it is also only with women. Of course there are also women who are super flirtatious or libertines who when they are paid go to dance at the *antros* on weekends.

"No, mama, now I have someone to defend me. Kevin at times is a bit rebellious but he listens to me, because he know has a girlfriend and he asks me permission to go and see her. And I tell him not to go out. And a little while later, he says, 'If I have done what you asked?' 'You finished your homework?' 'I don't need to do homework. I already know everything the teacher left for us. Why, then, won't you give me permission to go out?'"

"What does Irvin say?"

"Ay, mama, this kid lives in his own world. He is always working on his drawings and designs. He does not know if it is raining or windy outside. At times when I come back from work he is deeply asleep, waiting for me to make him something to eat. Because when Mundo makes food for them, he is always grumbling to them. And Irvin says he prefers going to sleep until I arrive, so he can eat comfortably."

"Listen Aida. Why have you put up with all of this? Now he is even disturbing your children."

"Mama, you know why I am putting up with him? When my children were little they closed off my world, because I didn't know who to leave them with so I could go out to look for work. And I was afraid he would do something to me in the middle of the street. And now I have told him that if he continues to be the same way, I will leave him. The good thing is that I now have a place to live and before I had no way of defending myself but now I have someone to protect me if he wants to do anything. Because of this I stay, and I don't want my offspring to reproach me one day."

"You know, Aida, they may reproach you someday, because you let him hit you in front of them. And don't tell me he didn't hit you. Remember when Irvine was a little baby and you came to the house with tears in your eyes? And how can you say you had no one to leave your children with so that you could look for work? What about us, who have always supported you? And I cared for the children of Indira and those of Magali, and I would have taken care of yours as well. I was always read to take care of my grandchildren. Moreover, remember that I even took care of Luisito, Toño's son, when Toño brought him to me at the age of two months--then, why not yours? But you are like me, who put up with the punches your father gave me. But I was right, because I had no one to protect me when we moved from Rosarito to Tijuana and then Mexicali. In Rosarito you father was tricky enough not to hit me where it showed. And in order not to mortify your grandparents, I didn't say anything to them. I

202

didn't have anyone's support, and even less so in Tijuana and Mexicali. But you, Aida, when I have always supported you?"

"Because I didn't know, mama, if my siblings were going to get involved and he would make problems for them as well, because even Mundo's siblings would not have remained quiet about it. And for this reason, I didn't say anything. No longer, mama, I am no longer so sweet."

Aida had three sons, the eldest now aged 20, and the little girl who on the 12th of November 2015 will be 13 years old.

My daughter, Aida Karelia, the youngest of my three daughters, in spite of her fragileness or delicateness, did go to work to help her husband with the household expenses. She went to work in a *maquiladora* as a line operator. I am not exactly sure what she made, but she earned minimum wage. But over time, and because of her perseverance, she was promoted to line supervisor, earning a bit more money. Also they are given extra for punctuality and she can work overtime if the *maquiladora* requires it. It is a *maquiladora* where only women work and I believe it is called "Panasonic." The truth is I don't know how much she earns because I have never liked to go about being an inquisitor. I know the above because at times she and my other daughter, Magali, talk about how things go at work and since Magali talks very loudly, I can't avoid hearing.

Magali works in another *maquiladora*. She also began as a line operator--as do all the *maquiladora* workers. There the workers make cases for all types of musical instruments. They are foreign *maquiladoras* that come to Mexico and I suppose invest their money and pay their workers as a cheap labor force. They pay 70 pesos a day, which seems to me a ridiculously low wage. But my daughter

Magali, after having worked there almost 20 years, was advanced to the post of supervisor. But it wasn't easy according to what she told me. She had to jump over many hurdles to get the post. She is the only woman supervisor alongside 7 men and she has to be careful of them because they lay traps for her so that she will be fired.

And it is not because they are my daughters, but I taught them to be honest in whatever employment they had. They have given Magali prizes for her perseverance at her work. She earns a bit more than Aida because they now pay more than the minimum wage. The truth is I don't know how much because I have never liked going around asking questions. I know they are earning well because the two of them start talking about the work. That is how I know, and also what expenses they have. Like Magali is paying off her house that she got through INFONAVIT and it is paid from her wages, that the I.M.S.S. withholds. Well, she has but a little money left over. But she has another little source of money. On weekends she goes to a market and sells second-hand clothing and whatever she has in the house that is not needed, she goes and sells it. Thus she obtains a little extra money. She also has expenses for her two daughters. The eldest is at the point of graduating from the university as a teacher, and the youngest is in secondary school. And when she has good sales she comes to my house and shares her profits with me.

My daughter Aida does the same thing. Even though she earns less than Magali, she gives me a little bit of money. But Aida has more children and the eldest is also studying in the university, and the only girl is studying in secondary school [junior high school] and the other two boys in preparatory [high school]. Even though Aida is married her husband sometimes lacks for work, because his craft is repairing electronic apparatuses. He doesn't always have work but they are helping their children move forward with their schooling.

And although Magali is living in free union with a man who is not the father of her daughters, he helps her economically and loves my granddaughters as though he were their father. Magali and her husband both work at the same factory, he as head of the line and she as supervisor. She seems very strict with her subordinates to him and it seems to him as well, that she goes around looking angry. But she answers him, "Juan, I have to look angry so that they obey! But you know if they ask for a day off for some reason, I do not deny it to them, and if I went around laughing with all of them, they would not take me seriously. Because you well know I do not stop working and supervising so that all will go well, because I am responsible if the work turns out badly. And I don't care what the other supervisors say. I obey my boss."

As concerns my sons: Antonio is a carpenter and makes furniture; Carlos works in the United States driving tractor trailers and is married to a woman born in Fresno and brought up in Calexico, where they live; Marcelo is presently working in a *maquiladora* and has previously worked in a casino and in foundries; Gustavo works in a *maquiladora* called "Sunpower," and Guillermo, my youngest, is studying industrial engineering in the university. I want him to be an engineer so that he goes to work and maintains me when I am older!

This was the true story of my life and hopefully it will serve as an example for those women who do not dare to speak up.

And such was my struggle or social labor as leader for my *colonia* from 1985 to 1992 in order to obtain a residential lot for my family though an invasion of lands. Now

I can say with pride that yes, one could (*sí, se pudo*). We have all the necessary services now though we are lacking in pavement. I hope we will have it in the future.

Epilogue

From the time the Unión de Residentes Lázaro Cárdenas was established in 1982, residents battled with the muddy roads that became flooded during the rainy season. People put on boots, if they had them, to navigate the slippery streets. People who had cars found themselves stuck in at least a foot of mud, and many had their car engines burn out as they tried to leave the colonia to go to work, or to buy groceries, to seek medical aid, or for any other reason.

In July of 2016, Ernestina formed a group of colonia residents, in an attempt to pressure the government to put in pavement, for which each of the residential lots would contribute funds, as they had for the electrical, water, and sewerage infrastructure. The group negotiations with the government led to demands that all lots pay their sewerage bill (electricity and water bills had to be paid before a sewerage system was put in) before the government would consider paving the colonia. So Ernestina and members of the group she had recruited went to more government offices in order to assure ease of payment for the very poor who had not had the funds to pay for sewerage to be extended to their lots. That took several months, and then at the end of the year, the government officials were to change, based on the 2016 election results.

Thus Ernestina--ever the activist and accompanied by the other activists in the colonia--plans to present the colonia's petitions for pavement to the new government officials in 2017. Now in her mid-60s, her story as an activist continues.

Glossary

Please note: If an acronym is spelled without periods between the letters, it is pronounced as if it were a word

Antros: discotheques, night clubs

Atole: drink made from corn meal, and usually sweetened

Birria: goat cooked in red chili sauce; usually served during parties to celebrate birthdays, *quinceañeras*, and weddings among other transition events

Bolillo: a white bread roll with a thick crust, used for sandwiches; it was introduced to Mexico by the French

Bracero: A person contracted to work under the U.S.-Mexico Bracero Program of 1942 to 1964; the workers were usually, though not exclusively, employed in the agricultural fields and *bracero* roughly translates as "field hand"

Buñuelos: fried wheat bread sticks covered in sugar, usually eaten at Christmas

C.C.I.: Central Campesino Independiente, Independent Peasants' Central; originally established to represent the interests of small farmers, it expanded to represent the interests of squatter settlement residents as well

C.E.S.P.M: Comisión Estatal de Servicios Públicos de Mexicali, Mexicali State Commission of Public Services: among its other missions, it provides legal advice to low income people

C.F.E.: Comisión Federal de Electricidad, Federal Electricity Commission; the federal agency responsible for providing electricity to the populace

Colonia: a named neighborhood within a city

Colonias populares: working-class neighborhoods; *colonias* formed through land invasions

Comadre: co-mother; ritual kinship relationship (female) established on the occasion when one of the two families' children is made godchild to another family. It can be established for any number of occasions but is most usual for baptisms, confirmations, weddings, and *quinceañeras*; once this co-parenthood relationship is established the *compadres* are expected to show the utmost respect to one another and romantic relationships are to be avoided even among their children

Comité de Vecinos: neighborhood committee; formed to represent the interests of a *colonia* at government offices

Compadre: co-father; ritual kin (male)

Compadres: May include a number of males who are co-parents or both *comadres* and *comadres*

Coyote: people smuggler

Don: Honorific used during the Colonial period in Mexico by the underclasses for the rich and powerful; contemporaneously used by the poor and working classes for any elderly man

Doña: Female version of *don*; used contemporaneously by the poor and working classes for any elderly woman and between older friends and *comadres* when respect is to be shown to the person addressed

Dorados: "the Golden ones;" the name supporters of Pancho Villa gave to his soldiers

Escuela Digna: part of the *Prospera* program initiated under President Enrique Peña Nieto (2012-2018), as a continuance and amplification of the *Progresa/Oportunidades* programs; under the *Escuela Digna* component, funds were provided to upgrade school buildings and provide shade over school courtyards; this was especially important in the *colonias populares* where schools were often built by the *colonia* residents of discarded materials

Ejido: communally owned, often individually tenured rural lands reinstated after the Mexican Revolution (1910-1917); prior to changes in Article 27 of the Mexican Constitution in 1992 (under President Salinas de Gortari), these lands could not legally by sold or mortgaged; also, a community where lands are held in common, whether worked communally or individually

Ejidatario: member of an *ejido* community who possesses *ejido* lands

Hija: daughter; *mi hija* (my daughter) is often used as a term of affection by husbands to wives or by non-family members to a girl or woman they feel affection for; plural, *hijas*

Hijo: son; *mi hijo* (my son) may be used as a term of affection for a boy or man

Hijos: sons or sons and daughters

Gorda, la: feminine for chubby one; a nickname often given to a girl by her husband or family

Gordo, el: masculine for chubby one; a nickname often given to a boy by his wife or family

IFE: Instituto Federal Electoral, Federal Electoral Institute; provides identification cards to potential voters; *IFE* is also the name of this identification card

IMSS: Instituto Mexicano de Seguro Social, Mexican Social Security Institute; an institution providing medical attention and pensions to workers in the informal economy; funded by payroll taxes, employer contributions, and the federal government.

INAPAM: Institution Nacional de Adultos Mayores, National Institute for Elderly Adults; provides an identification card to adults over 60 which permits them a discount on property taxes, medical supplies, water bills, and public transportation

Inmobilaria del Estado: State Real Estate Office, charged with property regulation, mapping, and taxation

INFONAVIT: Fonda Nacional de la Vivienda para los Trabajadores, National Fund for Workers' Housing; provides housing to workers in the formal economy through a tripartite system of payroll taxes and employer and federal government contributions

Jefa (f.), jefe (m.): chief, head of the tribe or family; a term of praise for one's mother or father

Lázaro Cárdenas: Mexican president from 1934 to 1940. The most left-wing of all Mexican presidents, he distributed more land to the *ejidos* than any president before and after him and nationalized key industries, such as petroleum. The petroleum industry was not privatized until 2014.

L.E.A.: Liga Agraria Estatal, State Agrarian League; a precursor to C.C.I. in Baja California

Ley Federal de Trabajo: Federal Labor Law, available in book form

Machetero: cane-cutter; wielder of a machete

Machista: A man who acts very *macho*, demeaning their wives, lording over their children, and

   womanizing

Macho: male, with connotations of unfairness toward women and those he considers his underlings

Mamí: mommy, affectionate term for mama

Mañanitas, las: traditional Mexican birthday song

Maquiladora: foreign-owned assembly plants first established in 1965 on the Mexican

   side of the U.S.-Mexico border; although established to give employment to men after the

   closure of the Bracero Program in 1964, they hire primarily women; contemporaneously there

   are *maquiladoras* in other parts of Mexico

Memo, Memito: nickname for Guillermo

Menudo: A popular soup made from cow's stomach

Niño Díos: God child; Jesus

Nixtamal: ground corn flour for making tortillas

Oportunidades: a conditional cash transfer program , under which mothers meet certain obligations

   in exchange for income to keep their children in school and insure their nutritional and health

   status. It was originally established in 1997 under the name of *Progresa* during the

   administration of President Ernesto Zedillo, former Secretary of Education.

PAN: Partido Acción Nacional, National Action Party. The most right wing of modern Mexican

   political parties and a supporter of big business; President Vincente Fox (2000-2006), the first

   president since the Mexican Revolution that did not belong to the PRI or to its precursor

Papí: daddy, with affection

Papíro: slang used by child vendors in Mexicali for "newspaper"

Patrón: boss, employer; land owner who employs workers; plural: *patrones;* feminine, *patrona*

Peon: worker, especially agricultural workers

Pendeja (f.): stupid, idiot; lit. pubic hair; masculine, *pendejo*

Peso: monetary unit in Mexico; in 2015, there was an average of between 15 and 16 *pesos* to a U.S.

> dollar

Piñatas: paper maché figures filled with candy; children, blindfolded, attempt to hit the *piñatas*

> with poles until the candy falls out, and all run to gather it up

Preparatoria: high school; grades 10 to 12

PRI: *Partido Revolucionario Institucional,* Institutional Revolutionary Party, established after the

> Mexican Revolution of 1910-1917; originally called the *Partida Nacional Revolucionario.* It

> was the ruling party in Mexico until the election of President Vicente Fox of the PAN in

> 2000, and recuperated its leading role afterwards

Priista: supporter of the PRI party

Prospera: the program replacing *Oportunidades* under the administration of President Enrique Peña

> Nieto (2012-2018); while continuing the cash transfer program, *Prospera* amplified some of

> the benefits and began giving scholarships for low-income university students

Quinceañera: A fifteen-year-old girl; a party for a fifteen-year old girl; it was long the custom to

> let girls begin seeing a boyfriend after reaching that age, and was essentially a "coming out"

> party

Rancho: an unincorporated rural settlement that can be populated with from 3-4 to 100 or more

> families; many *ranchos* contain *ejido* lands; alternatively, a ranch

Rodinos: label used by Mexicans, amnestied or not, to designate those who qualified for amnesty

> under the 1986 Immigration and Reform Control Act, also known as the Simpson-Rodino Act

> because of its sponsorship by Senator Alan K. Simpson and Representative Peter Rodino; the

> people in the *colonia* who became *Rodinos*, qualified under the Special Agricultural Workers

provision—many crossed the border illegally to work in the agricultural fields in the Imperial

Valley, and some, seasonally, went as far north as Salinas and Watsonville, California

SARH: Secretaría de Agricultura y Recursos Hídraulicos, Secretariat of Agriculture and Hydraulic

Resources

Secundaria: junior high school; grades 7 through 9

SEMEFO: Servicio Medico Forense, Forensic Medical Services; a murder investigation unit

Señora: a polite way of referring to or addressing a woman who is assumed to be married

Señor: a polite way of addressing or referring to a man

SEP: Secretaría de Educación Pública, Secretariat of Public Education

Soldaderas: the women who accompanied Pancho Villa's troops and cooked, sewed, and cleaned

for the male soldiers

SOLIDARIDAD: a poverty alleviation program initiated by President Carlos Salinas de Gortari

(1988-1994); one of its aims was squatter settlement regulation and upgrading

Sonido: sound machine with loudspeakers originally to play cassettes, nowadays to play CD's.

Tianguis: open air market usually open only a few days each week; a swap meet

Tienda de raya: company store, famous on the haciendas prior to the Mexican Revolution; the

peons who worked at the hacienda often became so deeply indebted to the *tienda de raya* that

they could never repay their debts and their children inherited them

Tocada: jam session

Toño: nickname for Antonio (Anthony)

Ernestina's house, built over the decades, as it has been since 2014